The Promise of the Third Day

YOUR DAY OF DESTINY HAS ARRIVED

The Promise
of the Third Day

YOUR DAY OF DESTINY HAS ARRIVED

BRUCE D. ALLEN

DESTINY IMAGE® PUBLISHERS, INC.
P.O. Box 310, Shippensburg, PA 17257-0310

*"Speaking to the Purposes of God for this Generation
and for the Generations to Come."*

This book and all other Destiny Image, Revival Press, Mercy Place, Fresh Bread, Destiny Image Fiction, and Treasure House books are available at Christian bookstores and distributors worldwide.

For a U.S. bookstore nearest you, call 1-800-722-6774.
For more information on foreign distributors, call 717-532-3040.
Or reach us on the Internet: www.destinyimage.com

ISBN 10: 0-7684-2492-5
ISBN 13: 978-0-7684-2492-8

For Worldwide Distribution, Printed in the U.S.A.

1 2 3 4 5 6 7 8 9 10 11 / 09 08 07

DEDICATION

I dedicate this work to my father and best friend, Ed Allen, who mentored me; my mother, Shirley Allen, who encouraged me; and especially my wife, Reshma, who believed in me. This book has been a labor of love and commitment to the direction of the Lord.

ACKNOWLEDGMENTS

I want to acknowledge and thank the many who were excited with me and contributed to this book in prayer and in time. Thank you, Faye Higbee, for your many hours of editing. Thank you, Therese Marszalek, for your continued encouragement and input into this process. Thank you, Pastors Barry and Kay Hill, for allowing me to spend five nights one December in teaching and expounding on this subject—this time gave greater clarity to verbalize the truths written here. Thank you to the many who have been eagerly anticipating and awaiting the completion of this book. Here it is!

ENDORSEMENTS

The Promise of the Third Day by Bruce Allen is chock-full of precious nuggets of revelation that must be received and understood by the Church if we are going to walk in the "high calling" of God.

> *"Eye has not seen, nor ear heard, nor have entered into the heart of man the things which God has prepared for those who love Him. BUT God has revealed them to us through His Spirit"* (1 Corinthians 2:9-10a).

These secrets are not revealed to everyone. Bruce Allen is one of the vessels through whom the Spirit of God has revealed many things that are about to take place. The Church would do well to discover what God is up to.

Pastor Joe Sweet
Shekinah Worship Center
Lancaster, California

A powerful, inspiring, and revelatory book that you will want to read and study again and again. In this chaotic world it is all too easy for understanding to be obscured and revelation from the Word of God to be scorned. This book offers biblical truth and evidence that we are in the very beginnings of the Third Day. It will also challenge and motivate you to discard the old habits that hold you back in your journey with the Lord.

The Promise of the Third Day is a treasure that will change your life.

Pastor T. Edward Allen
Real Life Christian Center
Wildomar, California

Bruce D. Allen has been a personal friend of my wife and mine for many years. Throughout our friendship, we've watched as God continually takes Bruce to new dimensions in the Spirit. He has a unique way of bringing fresh revelation of the realms of which we are to cooperate with in the days ahead. As God does this, Bruce processes it and then releases others in the Body of Christ to apprehend it for themselves, which we have personally experienced. *The Promise of the Third Day*, contains keys that will unlock these Kingdom mysteries for God's people to fulfill their own purpose through impartation, experience, and practice "for such a time as this."

John Filler
Apostolic Team, The Gateway
Coeur d'Alene, Idaho

We are living in a kiros moment in time, full of opportunities to advance the Kingdom of God. This is a time fore-ordained by God that is pregnant with destiny. There are specific promises that the Lord has given to this generation that are unlike any other promises released to previous generations. As we enter into the new millennium, the Lord is awakening us to our destinies in Him. God is making us aware of what is possible. Truly, the sky is the limit!

In this book, *The Promise of the Third Day*, Dr. Bruce Allen is releasing "Throne Room Revelation" for this hour. As you read you will be encouraged that you are here, not by mistake, but you have been brought to the Kingdom "for such a time as this."

I wholeheartedly endorse this book! It will cause you to better recognize the hour in which we are living as well as encourage you to pursue the Lord and His promises with a vengeance! Praise God we have entered into *The Promise of the Third Day*!

André Ashby
Soul's Cry Ministries

CONTENTS

PREFACE

THE LORD IS RELEASING INCREASED UNDERSTANDING AND REVELATION concerning the day and the hour in which we live. Truly we are a unique generation that will model and demonstrate the Kingdom of Heaven to a lost and perishing world. There is much work to be done before the advent of the Millennial Kingdom of Christ on earth. He will see it accomplished through an apostolic and a prophetic end-time people who have prepared themselves according to the strategies of Heaven being revealed and released through His Word.

I believe one of the keys to understanding these strategies is to know what the Word says concerning this time in history. Second Peter 3:8 says, "*with the Lord one day is as a thousand years, and a thousand years as one day.*" We have completed two days or two thousand years since the time of Christ. We are now living in a period of time foretold by the prophets of old: the Third Day.

Above any other generation, we are to be envied in our placement here by God at the end of the age. We, as an end time people, will witness untold miracles, signs, and wonders in this hour beyond anything we could ever imagine!

The revelation in this book was received over a five-year period, as the Lord released greater understanding and revelation. You will find confirmation, insight, and a greater sense of destiny as you read the pages of this book. I am convinced your life will be challenged and changed.

INTRODUCTION

THE PROPHET DANIEL SERVED IN THE COURT OF NEBUCHAD-
NEZZAR during the Babylonian Empire. As he stood by the
River Ulai, an apocalyptic vision of the end of time fell upon him.
While the fear of the Most High God enveloped him, angelic visitation provided interpretation. His experience, coupled with the
Revelation of John the Beloved on the Island of Patmos, rush
toward fulfillment in our day. What was sealed then for the time
of the end, is revealed now as we are thrust headlong into living
prophecy!

As we face the final summation of the ages, the church is
transformed into the prophetic church of Joel. Transformation of
the church requires both knowledge and a willingness to change.
Enter now a Scriptural "journey" through the preparation of the
promises for the Third Day!

Anonymous

CHAPTER ONE

SOWING AND REAPING

A Quick Harvest on the Third Day

FEAR SPREADS LIKE CANCER on nearly every continent. Terrorists paralyze and destroy entire populations. Governments dissolve into genocidal wars. Thousands die in horrific natural disasters. Medical science floods the world daily with hundreds of breakthrough drugs and treatments, while vaccine shortages and new strains of disease threaten the health of millions. The staggering pace of modern society bombards us in every newscast, from deep divisions over morality issues, to technological advancements. What does this plethora of change mean? Is there a reason or some explanation for the chaos around us?

Yes! Everything that happens throughout our society and the world is foretold within the covers of the Bible. We live at a unique juncture in history—the period just prior to the glorious return of Jesus Christ. As the world rushes toward the abyss, we are about to see the revelation and release of the mature sons and daughters of God foretold in the Word of God. (See Romans 8:19.)

The Word of God reveals a clear picture of the church and its transformation in these last days. We, as a generation, are about to see the Lord's vision of the church manifested in this final hour. This is that time, the moment in history that is both prophetic by nature and astounding by implication. The Glorious Church, the Spotless Bride of Christ, arises now…and we can be part of it! This hour holds the revelation of all that the Holy Spirit chooses to release to us, if we have "ears to hear" and "eyes to see."

A number of years ago the Lord began to challenge me regarding the "Third Day" as written in Scripture. It was new territory for me, and it tested some of my most cherished traditional thinking. I am astonished at the ability we have as people to cling to mind-sets that are currently popular yet very contrary to the Word of God.

The first place Holy Spirit led me was to Second Peter 3:8 *"But, beloved, do not forget this one thing, that with the Lord one day is as a thousand years, and a thousand years as one day."*

This is the foundational Scripture upon which the promise of the Third Day is based. From this inauspicious starting point, I embarked upon a journey of discovery that was both breathtaking and awe inspiring in its scope. The Word of God has an incredible amount to say about the Third Day and revelation pours forth to an overwhelming degree if we are willing to hear.

Before we begin, we must understand something about numbers in Scripture; they are supernatural in design and spiritual in significance. There is much revelation to be gleaned from the understanding of biblical numerology.

The number 3 is the number of the Godhead; Father, Son and Holy Spirit. It speaks of maturity and resurrection. It is the Third Day.

When we see the number 7 in the Bible, it is a prophetic picture and revelation of God's finished, perfect work. It speaks of completion and covenant promise fulfilled.

Think about the way Peter emphasized the "one thing" he didn't want the believers to forget. Don't forget this one thing! That is a powerful and sobering statement. Suppose Jesus Himself walked into the room right now and said to you, "I have just one thing I want you to remember above all else." You would know that there was weight and importance attached to that statement, wouldn't you?

When Peter says, "...*with the Lord one day is as a thousand years, and a thousand years as one day...*" it is my opinion that this Scripture was more for this generation than any other generation that preceded us. This is the end of the age.

From the time of Adam until approximately October 1999, we have completed six days and we've entered into the seventh day (more than 6,000 years, and moving into the 7,000th year). We have to understand from the outset, that the seventh day is a day of completion, a day of rest, a day of covenant promises being fulfilled and a day when the Lord will bring to conclusion all He began in the Garden of Eden. It is a day when the Lord spoke and said, "It is finished."

This is the seventh day, and the Lord is about to bring a magnificent, miraculous conclusion to everything He began! God has bestowed honor upon us in that we are alive and present at the conclusion of history! We cannot begin to comprehend how blessed we are. Picture it! In the strategy room of Heaven, before He laid the foundation of the world, the Father, the Son, and Holy Spirit, chose you and I to participate in the greatest event in the history of the world—the final harvest and return of Christ. The idea is overwhelming. The honor is incalculable. What an awesome God we serve!

If the President of the United States invited you to the White House to dine with him and the First Lady, you would feel honored, and rightly so. The One I am referring to is the King of the universe! And He says, "I want you, My chosen people, to see Me in My finest hour when I bring to conclusion every word and fulfill every vision; and I want you to be there to see it and participate in it!" This is the hour in which we live.

There is another significant number revealed at this time. From Jesus' birth to approximately October 1999, we have completed the second day, and we are now early in the morning of the third day (more than 2,000 years and moving into the 3,000th year). These two days relate prophetically to the day in which we live—they reveal a specific design and purpose of the Savior. As we continue to delve into this prophetic picture we will see more clearly the profound implications of what it means to live on planet Earth as these prophetic days unfold before us.

THE THIRD DAY

The Third Day is the day of resurrection, and it signifies a release of resurrection power in this hour. That is why we have been hearing and will continue to hear more and more testimonies about people being raised from the dead. It's the day of resurrection! This is a profound prophetic picture and witness of the hour in which we live. Jesus was our forerunner not only literally but in type also. There are more people being raised from the dead in this hour than any other time in history. An American missionary in Mexico has seen in his ministry alone close to 200 people raised from the dead.

The Word clearly states that Jesus is also Lord of the Sabbath (see Luke 6:5). The Sabbath is the seventh day. While we know that Jesus is Lord of all, there is a special impetus and weight to Jesus' statement of being Lord of the Sabbath, the seventy (seventh) day, in which we live. His Lordship will be demonstrated and displayed to an extent and to a degree the world has never seen. And it will be displayed in and through the Body of Christ.

As we study the Word of God we find that divine covenants appear to be established at 2,000 year intervals. You will find that the Abrahamic covenant was established approximately 2,000 years after the fall of Adam and Eve. The blood of Christ instituted the "New Covenant" or "New Testament" approximately 2,000 years after the covenant of Abraham. Right now we stand 2,000 years from that New Covenant. Clearly, we are on the threshold of the most wondrous move of God the world has ever seen!

> "Many spiritual Jews have long divided the six-day work week God gave Adam like this (using 1,000 years as a day): Two days of chaos. Two days of the law. Two days of Messiah. Then would come the seventh day of rest.
>
> They correctly saw that the Messiah would come after four days—after 4,000 years. (They believe that He did not come because they were not ready.) The two days of His rule, being the last of the three periods, were called the last days.
>
> When Jesus came 2,000 years ago, it was the beginning of the last days. We live at the end of the last days."[1]

Ancient Rabbinical history indicates that Jewish rabbis understood Adam had only been given a six-day lease on the earth. It was irrelevant that he allowed satan to wrest control of this earth from him. The lease was still only six days. It was foretold by rabbis that on the seventh day the Lord would reclaim the earth and all that He created. He will not wait until the end of the seventh day to do so, as we will discover.

This promise of the Third Day is revealed as we journey through Scripture. Every verse we examine has a corresponding ministry application as well as a personal application and fulfillment associated with the work of the Holy Spirit in us and through us. The Lord taught me a long time ago that *what He chooses to release **through** us must first be formed **in** us*. The truth about the Third Day must be received by faith and by the revelation of the Holy Spirit. Once the revelation is formed in us we will begin to walk in these promises, and the Lord will be glorified through us. We must walk in these promises; we must work out our sanctification. We must come to the place where the character of Christ is exemplified in our lives rather than the worthless works of our flesh. The church has been inundated for generations with fleshly carnal character that portrays a less-than-truthful picture of Christ. This is the hour when the Lord will return for a church without spot or wrinkle, a mature, spotless church. What an honor…and what a sobering thought!

SEPARATION OF THE BODY FOR CHANGE

The first third day Scripture is found in Genesis 1:9-13.

Then God said, "Let the waters under the heavens be gathered together into one place, and let the dry land appear"; and it was so. And God called the dry land Earth, and the

24

*gathering together of the waters He called Seas. And God
saw that it was good. Then God said, "Let the earth bring
forth grass, the herb that yields seed, and the fruit tree that
yields fruit according to its kind, whose seed is in itself, on
the earth;" and it was so. And the earth brought forth grass,
the herb that yields seed according to its kind, and the tree
that yields fruit, whose seed is in itself according to its kind.
And God saw that it was good. So the evening and the
morning were the third day.*

Our God is a creative God. The only thing in this universe,
the only thing in all of creation that does not change is God.
Everything else is in a constant state of flux and change. You and
I were created for conflict and change. Your physical body must
constantly challenge itself. From muscles to mental faculties,
without continual stimuli and challenge, you will atrophy and
wither away to nothing. You and I were created for change and
conflict. Nature itself proves this. None of us were created to be
couch potatoes or pew warmers.

There is no such thing as spectator Christianity. Rather I
should say, spectatorship was never God's plan for His people.
Our traditions and our fears have created vicarious involvement,
rather than proactive participation. None of us are called to be
spectators in the end of the age! The watchmen on the wall, the
intercessors, are not to be spectators, they are the gatekeepers
who must man their post and sound the alarm as God gives them
command.

You will notice in Genesis 1:9, that the waters were "gathered
together into one place, and the dry land appeared." There is a
very serious prophetic picture in this one verse. "Throughout
Scripture water or waters speak of either peoples or the nations of

the earth; restlessness, undercurrents, crosscurrents or eternal life and the Holy Spirit flowing."[2]

Earth or dust is what man was created from in Genesis 2:7. It speaks of the flesh or the works of the flesh. From this we can glean that on the Third Day, there is going to be a separation of that which is of the flesh and that which is of the Spirit. Not only has the arm of flesh not ever accomplished and fulfilled the plans and purposes of God, but on this day it will be exposed for what it truly is, flesh. We will begin to see a clear demarcation between the works of the flesh and that which is truly of the Spirit!

Today's headlines show restlessness in the world. The undercurrents, the crosscurrents of change give us a natural picture of the supernatural separation now underway. There will be a separation within the church itself as this Third Day advances, and there will be a separation in the world as the earth races toward destruction. Unity will come to the Body of Christ as those who are led by the Spirit of God position themselves according to the voice of the Lord and surrender their agendas for the strategies of Heaven! This will be the "waters" gathering together in one place bringing forth a unity in the Body of Christ that has eluded us for centuries. There is a separation and transformation of the individual believer as the Lord turns up the heat to cause us to reflect upon what is in our heart and to examine ourselves in the light of His glory. The dross always comes to the surface when the furnace is alight!

SOWERS AND REAPERS

"Behold, the days are coming," says the Lord, "When the plowman shall overtake the reaper, and the treader of

grapes him who sows seed; The mountains shall drip with sweet wine, and all the hills shall flow with it" (Amos 9:13).

The Lord says that the days are at hand and we will see the fulfillment of every vision according to Ezekiel 12. No longer will His Word be postponed, but there will be a complete fulfillment of every Word of God to us and to this generation.

And the word of the Lord came to me, saying, "Son of man, what is this proverb that you people have about the land of Israel, which says, 'The days are prolonged, and every vision fails'? Tell them therefore, 'Thus says the Lord God: "I will lay this proverb to rest, and they shall no more use it as a proverb in Israel." But say to them, "The days are at hand, and the fulfillment of every vision. For no more shall there be any false vision or flattering divination within the house of Israel. For I am the Lord. I speak, and the Word which I speak will come to pass; it will no more be postponed; for in your days, O rebellious house, I will say the Word and perform it," says the Lord God'" (Ezekiel 12:21-25).

The seeds that we have to sow are the same seeds that God sowed when He spoke, and it came to pass. You and I are created in God's image and in His likeness, after His kind. He breathed into us the very breath of life, the "Ruach Ha Kodesh," or Holy Spirit. Therefore we have that impartation of the very Spirit of God. When we speak, creative power goes forth out of our mouths.

Understand, the reaper overtakes the sower in the last hour, and the seed that we sow grows quickly! Why? Because it is the seventh day...the conclusion of the plan of the Living God, He is doing a quick work in the earth as we race toward the fulfillment of His Word.

WATCH THE WORDS OF YOUR MOUTH!

Since late 1998 into 1999, I've observed that the prophetic word often manifests fulfillment within days or even hours of being spoken. For example, in a meeting I held in Coeur d'Alene, Idaho, I gave a woman a prophetic word, and within minutes she came back and shared with me how the Lord had just fulfilled that word via a phone call she had just received. You see, the reaper is overtaking the sower. We won't be able to sow the seed fast enough to keep ahead of the reaper, therefore we must be very aware of what we speak.

"*The sower sows the Word*" (Mark 4:14). We need to get this Scripture into our hearts. You are a sower, and you sow the Word. Not just God's Holy Word, the Bible, but every word that comes out of your mouth is a seed that is sown with creative power in it. You might say, wait a minute, I sow more than just words, I sow finances, time, energy, gifting, etc. That is true. However, your harvest is dependant upon your corresponding words—they are not only seed that is sown, but they also water the seed that has been sown.

"*You are snared by the words of your* [own] *mouth; You are taken by the words of your mouth*" (Prov. 6:2). This information is not new. But the principle is fresh, due to the day and hour in which we live. There is an added dimension, an added significance to the seed we sow in this the last day. What we sow, we will reap. Life or death, blessing or cursing; we will be snared by the words of our mouth!

Most assuredly, I say to you, he who believes in Me, the works that I do he will do also; and greater works than these he will do, because I go to My Father. And whatever you ask in My name, that I will do, that the Father may be glorified in the Son. If you ask anything in My name, I will do it (John 14:12-14).

Many of us have quoted this Scripture. We hope it causes the Lord to anoint us with power to accomplish signs wonders and miracles; so that we will ultimately be seen of men and make room for our ministry. What we fail to realize is that the first works that Jesus did had nothing to do with signs, wonders, or miracles. He learned obedience through the things He suffered (see Heb. 5:8). He became of no reputation and took the form of a bond-servant (see Phil. 2:7). He suffered temptation (see Heb. 2:18). He was reviled and did not revile in return (see 1 Pet. 2:21-23). These are the works that shaped Jesus' character to such an extent that the Father could entrust to Him all the authority of Heaven and release to Him the Spirit without measure. Jesus said that we would do the works that He did also. He laid down His life that others might live—in what way are we emulating Him in His "first works"?

Do not be deceived, God is not mocked; for whatever a man sows, that he will also reap. For he who sows to his flesh will of the flesh reap corruption, but he who sows to the Spirit will of the Spirit reap everlasting life. And let us not grow weary while doing good, for in due season we shall reap if we do not lose heart (Galatians 6:7-9).

There are some very poignant questions we must ask ourselves at this time. *What type of seed do we sow? What type of harvest will overtake us in this hour? What do we sow into the lives of those around us?* Do not be deceived, we will give an account for the words of our mouth.

In this Third Day, the Lord has been training and retraining His people to be very aware of what they speak, what they look upon, what they listen to, what they surround themselves with, where they go, etc. The responsibility required of us is greater today than previously. The seeds we sow today will reap a quick harvest now and in the future as well.

The following is a personal testimony of sowing the correct seed. In February 2001, the Lord began to speak to me that I was crowned with the unparalleled, unprecedented, unmerited favor of God. Each morning, I would confess what the Lord had revealed to me, that I was crowned with unparalleled, unprecedented, unmerited favor. I printed signs and framed them and put them up in my home to remind me of what the Lord was saying to me. I began to teach this message in various places, as the Lord would lead.

During that year, I was given a house, a Corvette, a motor home, and I was asked if I wanted a sailboat. The house needed remodeling, and I was given all the funds necessary to make the renovations. Was I special? No! It was my agreement with the word, and my actions that enforced my agreement. I sowed seed in accordance with that word. My confession was in agreement with what was in my heart, and I reaped a tremendous harvest.

The end of that story came in December 2001 while I was in Oklahoma City during Christmas and New Years. I began to seek the Lord and ask Him what He had in store for 2002. The Spirit of God spoke to me and said that 2002 was a "year of increase." I was astonished and dumbfounded! I couldn't conceive of anything else He might want to give me. An airplane? A cruise ship?

I just couldn't imagine what He was trying to tell me. So I asked Him what He wanted me to do to prepare for this increase. He said that I was to give everything away; all the blessings He had bestowed upon me that past year, the house, the car, the motor home, everything. So I did. And the increase was greater than I could have ever expected or imagined. He gave me my precious wife, Reshma. And the increase has not stopped since.

And they overcame him by the blood of the Lamb and by the word of their testimony, and they did not love their lives to the death (Revelation 12:11).

Notice there are three key points in this verse. *You overcome first and foremost by the blood of the Lamb.* In this day and hour, there will be tremendous revelation released regarding the blood of Jesus, and the power of that blood. Many have forgotten that knowledge. The old timers during Pentecost understood the power of the blood. The Spirit of God told them to use the blood to its fullest, and the blood would protect and fulfill them. There is nothing that can cross the bloodline if you apply it. We overcome by the blood of the Lamb! In any situation you face, you overcome by the blood of the Lamb and everything it purchased for you.

Second, *you overcome by the word of your testimony.* What is the word of your testimony today about any area of your life? Do the words of your testimony line up with the words of Jesus' testimony?

Therefore rejoice, O heavens, and you who dwell in them! Woe to the inhabitants of the earth and the sea! For the devil has come down to you, having great wrath, because he knows that he has a short time (Revelation 12:12).

The devil is enraged. His time is short. We need to understand and appropriate the covenant power in the blood of the

Lamb, and our testimony must reflect our faith in that shed blood. We overcome by the blood of the Lamb and the word of our testimony. What is your testimony today?

Third, *they loved not their lives even to death.* This is called the crucified life. I've heard it said that we are loose change in God's pocket and He can spend us anywhere He wishes. While this may seem trite, I believe it is time for the Body of Christ to develop a mind-set of servanthood. Jesus became of no reputation and took the form of a bondservant. Too often in the Church we vie for preeminence rather than esteeming others better than ourselves. Jesus Himself became obedient even unto death. How can we offer Him anything less? It is the image of Christ in us that we must emulate.

God's work in this Third Day is quick and amazing. The seeds we sow will not take years to for us to reap a harvest; but we will be harvesting for years what we sow today. We must understand who we are, what we are called to be and sow accordingly.

— *Let the redeemed of the Lord say so, Whom He has redeemed from the hand of the enemy* (Psalm 107:2).

If you and I are redeemed, we need to speak it! We are delivered and redeemed from the hand of all of our enemies.

For with the heart one believes unto righteousness, and with the mouth confession is made unto salvation (Romans 10:10).

Whatever you believe with your heart you will confess with your mouth because *"out of the abundance of the heart the mouth speaks"* (Matt. 12:34). It has become glaringly obvious that the majority of the Church believes anything but the Word of God.

A good man out of the good treasure of his heart brings forth good; and an evil man out of the evil treasure of his heart brings forth evil. For out of the abundance of the heart his mouth speaks (Luke 6:45).

What do we need salvation from today? What do we need the power of God to save us from today? *Our salvation is in direction proportion to our confession and our confession flows from what is deposited in our heart.*

Why is it that those who have walked the most with the Lord and have come to a place of maturity are the ones who speak the least? Because they understand that they are sowing and there will be a harvest. They understand the wisdom of refraining from trivial or idle conversation that has no life in it.

Remember James 1:19 and Proverbs 17:27-28: be slow to speak, slow to anger and quick to listen. I phrase it like this: "only speak when spoken through, only do what He tells you to do. Only go where He tells you to go and He will let you know what you need to know."

With your mouth sow only that which God tells you. Remember the swiftness of the harvest in this hour. Think about your words. And know that the blessings, the promises of God in your life are on the verge of fulfillment. This is the season of the fulfillment of every promise! That which you have stood for in faith over the years can be accomplished at any moment. As we search deeper into the Third Day prophetic message, you will begin to get a glimpse of the awesome harvest and season of promise that has opened before us.

In this hour, it would do well for us to meditate upon and understand the following Scriptures:

For whatever is born of God overcomes the world. And this is the victory that has overcome the world—our faith (1 John 5:4).

The fear of the LORD is to hate evil; Pride and arrogance and the evil way, and the perverse mouth I hate (Proverbs 8:13).

The mouth of the righteous is a well of life, But violence covers the mouth of the wicked (Proverbs 10:11).

The hypocrite with his mouth destroys his neighbor, But through knowledge the righteous will be delivered (Proverbs 11:9).

The words of the wicked are, 'Lie in wait for blood,' but the mouth of the upright will deliver them (Proverbs 12:6).

A man will be satisfied with good by the fruit of his mouth, And the recompense of a man's hands will be rendered to him (Proverbs 12:14).

A man shall eat well by the fruit of his mouth, But the soul of the unfaithful feeds on violence. He who guards his mouth preserves his life, But he who opens wide his lips shall have destruction (Proverbs 13:2-3).

A man has joy by the answer of his mouth, and a word spoken in due season, how good it is! (Proverbs 15:23).

The heart of the wise teaches his mouth, and adds learning to his lips (Proverbs 16:23).

A fool's mouth is his destruction, and his lips are the snare of his soul (Proverbs 18:7).

A man's stomach shall be satisfied from the fruit of his mouth, from the produce of his lips he shall be filled (Proverbs 18:20).

Death and life are in the power of the tongue, and those who love it will eat its fruit (Proverbs 18:21).

Whoever guards his mouth and tongue keeps his soul from troubles (Proverbs 21:23).

QUICK HARVEST

It was 1998 and my first trip to Fiji. On the first Sunday morning, as I walked up a hill to the church, I heard the word "earthquake" in my spirit. At first I thought it was my imagination, but that "still small voice" persisted. Three times, I heard "earthquake." When I got to the pulpit for my first meeting, the Lord spoke to my heart and said, "prophesy earthquake." He continued, "As a sign to you that Fiji is going to see revival, there will be an earthquake in the natural. It is a sign that I the Lord am going to shake up the established order in this country, first in the church and then in the natural." That was Sunday morning.

Sunday evening the Lord again quickened my spirit to prophesy and He said, "There is going to be a tropical storm that will cause widespread flooding and it is a sign to you of the outpouring of the Holy Spirit upon Fiji. People will come to Fiji, not for the sun, surf, and sand, but because of the move of God on this nation." I had no idea that Fiji had been in nine months of drought at that time.

Tuesday evening there was an earthquake. Two and a half days after the Lord spoke to me a small tsunami hit the coral coast as a result of the earthquake—a prophetic picture of the nations coming to the shores of Fiji.

On Thursday evening, it began to rain, and I was told later that it was a very unusual storm because it rained heavily on *all* of the islands of the archipelago rather than the usual handful.

Shortly after I left the country, the churches were in much upheaval as the Lord began to reveal and expose sin. Pastors were removed from ministry, and churches split as God revealed the motives of the hearts of His people. Two years later, in the year 2000, the president and parliament of Fiji was overthrown in a coup. By 2002, Fiji was in revival from one island to another.

That's how quickly the prophetic word came to pass. This is when the Lord began to teach me about the Third Day quick harvest and the release of His anointing on this generation.

Here is the key: when you speak when spoken through, God moves mightily to perform His word without the delay we once experienced, and the result is life. Conversely, when we speak according to our fleshly desires, or from the pressure of our circumstance, or when we react because of the situation we find ourselves in, the result can be death.

We overcome by the blood of the Lamb and the word of our testimony. Confession leads to salvation. What we speak bears fruit, and the reaper overtakes the sower. This is the Third Day.

ENDNOTES

1. Billye Brim, *The Blood and the Glory* (Tulsa, OK: Harrison House, 1995), 120-121.

2. Kevin Conner, *Interpreting The Symbols And Types* (Portland, OR: City Christian Publishing, 1999).

CHAPTER TWO

RETURN TO YOUR FIRST LOVE

The God of the Promise

I N ADDITION TO THE CONFESSION OF OUR LIPS, we must love the
God of the Promise more than the promise of God.

*Now it came to pass after these things that God tested
Abraham, and said to him, "Abraham!" And he said, "Here
I am." And He said, "Take now your son, your only son
Isaac, whom you love, and go to the land of Moriah, and
offer him there as a burnt offering on one of the mountains
of which I shall tell you." So Abraham rose early in the
morning and saddled his donkey, and took two of his young
men with him, and Isaac his son; and he split the wood for
the burnt offering, and arose and went to the place of
which God had told him. Then on the **third day** Abraham
lifted his eyes and saw the place afar off. And Abraham said
to his young men, "Stay here with the donkey; the lad and
I will go yonder and worship, and we will come back to
you." So Abraham took the wood of the burnt offering and
laid it on Isaac his son; and he took the fire in his hand,
and a knife, and the two of them went together. But Isaac
spoke to Abraham his father and said, "My father!" And he*

said, "Here I am, my son." Then he said, "Look, the fire and the wood, but where is the lamb for a burnt offering?" And Abraham said, "My son, God will provide for Himself the lamb for a burnt offering." So the two of them went together.

Then they came to the place of which God had told him. And Abraham built an altar there and placed the wood in order; and he bound Isaac his son and laid him on the altar, upon the wood. And Abraham stretched out his hand and took the knife to slay his son. But the Angel of the Lord called to him from Heaven and said, "Abraham, Abraham!" And he said, "Here I am." And He said, "Do not lay your hand on the lad, or do anything to him; for now I know that you fear God, since you have not withheld your son, your only son, from Me." Then Abraham lifted his eyes and looked, and there behind him was a ram caught in a thicket by its horns. So Abraham went and took the ram, and offered it up for a burnt offering instead of his son. And Abraham called the name of the place, The-Lord-Will-Provide; as it is said to this day, "In the Mount of the Lord it shall be provided" (Genesis 22:1-14).

You will notice that it was God who tested Abraham, not the devil. So often I've heard Christians say that God wouldn't test us, but that the devil or satan was attacking them. I find for myself that the majority of the trials in my life have their source in my flesh! Occasionally, I will find that the enemy is the one responsible for the trials or testing in my life, but this is not the most frequent scenario. It becomes obvious when the testing of God is at work because it has redemptive value. In this case we find Abraham being tested, not so the Lord can discover what is in his heart, but that Abraham himself will see the changes the Lord has brought about in his heart.

Verse two can be paraphrased this way: Take now the promise for your life, the ministry, the hope for a job and raise, the home, whatever the promise may be, take it now and go to the land of Moriah and offer it there to Me as a burnt offering upon the altar of sacrifice. (According to *Hitchcock's Bible Name Dictionary*, the name *Moriah* means "bitterness of the Lord.")

Most of us would argue with the voice of the Lord. "Why, God would never require of us the very thing we tenaciously believed for so long. After all, God would not give and take away like that." Yes, He would! Not only will the Lord require this of us, you will notice that it was Abraham who built his own altar. On this Third Day in our life we will be required to build our own altar of sacrifice to the Lord.

Then Abraham bound his son and laid him upon the altar. He took the knife and was about to offer up Isaac when the Angel of the Lord stopped him. In other words: "Do not lay your hand on the promise, or do anything to it; for now I know that you fear God, since you have not withheld your promised (fill in the blank), your only (fill in the blank), from Me."

On this day, the Third Day, the Lord is going to test our hearts to see if we love the God of the Promise more than the Promise of God. For too long the Church has made an idol of the ministry, the gifts, or the ministers at the altar rather than recognizing that God and God alone is to be worshiped. Too often we have made idols out of the blessings of the Lord—now we are required to recognize the Lord of the blessing. That is not to say that we cannot desire spiritual gifts. We are encouraged to do so (see 1 Cor. 14:1). But there must be balance in our lives, in every area of our lives. Realizing the difference between worshiping God and worshiping blessings is called maturity.

This place is called Mt. Moriah, the place of bitterness, where God tests us so that we will know what is in our hearts. *He allows us to find out whether we love the God of the promise more than the promise itself.* It's no accident that the Spirit of God has manifested in ministries such as the Harp and Bowl in Kansas City, or in messages such as The God Chasers where a passion for the heart of God is the focus—here the Third Day principle is being released by the Holy Spirit. God has taken the hearts of the children and turned them back to the Father. The prodigal is returning home! And we are that prodigal. (See Luke 15.)

Our focus and our passions have been everywhere except on the heart of the Father. God tests us because we are to become the Church without spot or wrinkle. From a lukewarm, self-centered gospel to the glorious Bride is a vast chasm of conformity to Christ. There is a long way for the Church to go to become what we are called to become. The very earth itself awaits the revelation of the mature sons of God. That calling is for us!

For the earnest expectation of the creation eagerly waits for the revealing of the sons of God (Romans 8:19).

But we must go by way of Mt. Moriah, where the dream, the hope, the vision, the passion, must be laid upon the altar of sacrifice. You cannot love the promise more than God Himself. He will know if you are sincere.

We find later in Scripture that Mt. Moriah is the location of Solomon's Temple. The very foundation of the temple was laid upon this revelation of loving the God of the promise more than the promise of God.

> *He who loves father or mother more than Me is not worthy of Me. And he who loves son or daughter more than Me is not worthy of Me. And he who does not take his cross and follow after Me is not worthy of Me. He who finds his life will lose it, and he who loses his life for My sake will find it* (Matthew 10:37-39).

He who loves ministry more than Christ is not worthy of Christ. He who loves son or daughter more than God is not worthy of God. He who loves position, or title, or possessions, you name it, more than Jesus, is not worthy of Jesus. He who does not take his cross and follow after Me is not worthy of Me. Paul said in First Corinthians 15:31 "*...I die daily.*" The church today needs a revelation of that Scripture. Today's church will be given the opportunity very shortly to embrace the heart of a true believer and follower of the Lord with our demonstration of "dying daily." We need to truly learn what it means to live the crucified life.

> *But Jesus said to him, "No one, having put his hand to the plow, and looking back, is fit for the kingdom of God"* (Luke 9:62).

> *So likewise, whoever of you does not forsake all that he has cannot be My disciple* (Luke 14:33).

We, as ministers, have perpetrated falsehood in the church. We are called to be followers of Christ, and we are called to become friends of God, but the truth is, we are not. Lip service is not faith in action. I came to the reality of this truth in my own life when the Lord revealed my heart to me. We have been a self-serving bunch of people looking out for our own interests with the attitude that God is here to serve us. This couldn't be farther from the truth. We speak what we say we believe, but we have to do more than speak; we have to act upon what we believe and what we speak. Faith without works is dead.

We are about to obtain the promises of God, not by any position we have held or tried to find, but by possession of them. The Word says that we are raised with Christ and sit with Him at the right hand of God.

> *If then you were raised with Christ, seek those things which are above, where Christ is, sitting at the right hand of God. Set your mind on things above, not on things on the earth. For you died, and your life is hidden with Christ in God* (Colossians 3:1-3).

> *...and raised us up together, and made us sit together in the heavenly places in Christ Jesus...* (Ephesians 2:6).

If this position is true, because God calls those things that are not as though they are, then why do we as Christians struggle so much with the things of this life? It is because we have not yet possessed the fullness of the promise of God in this area of our lives. This Third Day is the time when we will actually transition *from position to possession* of the reality of the Word of God.

These issues are foundational: *what we sow with our mouths*, and *who is our first love*. Once we deal with these issues, blessings begin to flow in an unprecedented way for the remainder of our Christian sojourn. Every other Third Day Scripture speaks of victory and blessing, as we are obedient to Him in this hour.

42

Understanding the foundations of Third Day manifestation is imperative:

1. We must be cognizant of what we speak and what we release with our mouths because the seed we sow is going to bring a quick harvest; and,

2. We must love the God of the promise more than the promise itself.

We will live with Him for all eternity, and realizing these principles now will prepare us for life eternal. The world has not yet seen the supernatural sons and daughters of the Living God—but that is about to change dramatically.

WORDS, LOVE, AND SUPERNATURAL VISITATION

Another aspect of the Third Day is the increase of angelic visitations and our interaction with the heavenly host. Quite frequently we see angelic activity in our meetings—including the presence of Michael and Gabriel. (How do I know it is Michael and Gabriel? I asked the Lord, and He told me.) I've witnessed Gabriel deliver scrolls with strategic messages and Third Day strategies to individuals and leaders who have been seeking the Lord for such.

In each instance when I witnessed Gabriel deliver his message, unequivocally every person who received it had fire come into their hand. In three out of the five instances, the instruction was to prophetically eat the scroll, and as they did the fire would burn within them for hours.

On one occasion we were ministering in a Lutheran Church. Our hosts, a husband and wife, sat in the back of the church next to a glass partition between the foyer and the sanctuary. As I shared the testimonies about Michael and Gabriel's visitations, Gabriel himself walked into the room. He stood next to our hosts, and I was instructed to have the husband hold out his right hand. As he held out his right hand, I saw Gabriel place the scroll in his hand. Abruptly, he was struck by the power of God and swayed, almost unable to stand. He staggered toward the window, and it appeared as if he might crash through it. I was then instructed to have him, as a prophetic gesture, place the scroll in his mouth and begin to eat it. As he did, he was unable to stand and fell back into his seat.

Next, he was instructed to give the scroll to his wife and she was to eat the scroll also. As she did, the power of God came upon her. They testified that the impartation continued for some time after the experience.

I share this angelic visitation because *supernatural strategies have been released in supernatural ways.* It is the prophetic mandate of the Third Day church and the prophetic word of the seventh day that releases us into the destiny that God foreordained for us to live out. As we study Third Day passages further we find that the Lord has released supernatural Third Day strategies to His people to take cities, regions, states, and nations.

Some of you have been frustrated for years. Just when you were about to obtain the promise, it was snatched from your reach. This will not happen again. Destiny is being released! We are being conformed to His image, and we are being released to perform exploits in the name of the Lord. The exhibition of the mature sons and daughters of God is for such a time as this.

The Lord said that we have dominion over all the works of His hands. That encompasses everything God created. He said the universe and everything He made fits in the span of His hand. He gave us authority over everything He created. My mind cannot grasp the scope of that statement. It is almost incomprehensible! We have a difficult time dealing with our own circumstances and issues, let alone trying to comprehend dominion and authority over everything that has been created. Yet that is what He is releasing to us in this hour.

Nature has heeded the authoritative voice of men and women of God who know who they are and where they stand. Death has heeded the voice and command of believers as they stand in their God-given authority. Creative miracles, signs, and wonders as well as signs in the heavens above and earth beneath burst forth as God releases His authority and destiny both in us and through us. You and I will witness the greatest finale in all of history. He has chosen us to participate with Him in the end of this age—all because of the love and grace of God.

It is time to return to our First Love, to allow His destiny for us to be fulfilled. We need to get excited and live in expectancy! As we grasp the concept of loving the God of the promise more than the promise of God we will be released into our destiny and see the fulfillment our calling spring forth. As we do, our words will match our walk and we will be fruitful in every area of our lives. No longer will we be enamored of those things that will perish, but we will be well on our way to an imperishable crown as we become overcomers during the days of darkness that are coming upon the earth. The release of our destiny is here!

Chapter Three

Promise and Warning

The Impure Heart Shall Not Speak Against You

I N THE FIRST TWO CHAPTERS, a basic foundation was established for the definition of the Third Day, and what is actually required of us. First, we must watch what we speak as it brings a quick harvest; and second, we must love the God of the promise more than the promise of God. Now we explore Scriptures that reveal more promises released to the Third Day covenant people—specific prophetic promises that will revolutionize our lives as we catch the revelation. We must decree these promises! Remember, confession is made unto salvation.

IMPURE HEARTS CANNOT HARM YOU

*And Laban was told on **the third day** that Jacob had fled. Then he took his brethren with him and pursued him for **seven days'** journey, and he overtook him in the mountains of Gilead. But God had come to Laban the Syrian in a dream by night, and said to him, "**Be careful that you speak to Jacob neither good nor bad.**" So Laban overtook Jacob. Now Jacob had pitched his tent in the mountains, and Laban with his brethren pitched in the mountains of*

Gilead. And Laban said to Jacob: "What have you done, that you have stolen away unknown to me, and carried away my daughters like captives taken with the sword? Why did you flee away secretly, and steal away from me, and not tell me; for I might have sent you away with joy and songs, with timbrel and harp? And you did not allow me to kiss my sons and my daughters. Now you have done foolishly in so doing. It is in my power to do you harm, but the God of your father spoke to me last night, saying, 'Be careful that you speak to Jacob neither good nor bad'" (Genesis 31:22-29).

Most of us know the story of Jacob who usurped the birthright of his brother Esau. Because he feared his brother's wrath, he fled his homeland. He worked as a laborer for Laban, who eventually became his father-in-law. The truth of sowing and reaping is evident here. Jacob deceived his brother Esau, and Laban deceived him. He worked 14 years in order to marry his wives Rachel and Leah, and then approximately another 7 years until he knew it was time for him to return home.

The story of Jacob is relevant to our journey on this Third Day. In Genesis 28, we find that Jacob had a visitation from the Lord while he slept.

Now Jacob went out from Beersheba and went toward Haran. So he came to a certain place and stayed there all night, because the sun had set. And he took one of the stones of that place and put it at his head, and he lay down in that place to sleep. Then he dreamed, and behold, a ladder was set up on the earth, and its top reached to Heaven; and there the angels of God were ascending and descending on it. And behold, the Lord stood above it and said: "I am the Lord God of Abraham your father and the God of Isaac; the land on which you lie I will give to you and your descendants. Also your descendants shall be as the dust of the earth; you shall spread abroad to the west and the east, to the north and the south; and in you and in your seed all the families of the earth shall be blessed. Behold, I am with you and will keep you wherever you go, and will bring you back to this land; for I will not leave you until I have done what I have spoken to you." Then Jacob awoke from his sleep and said, "Surely the Lord is in this place, and I did not know it." And he was afraid and said, "How awesome is this place! This is none other than the house of God, and this is the gate of Heaven!" Then Jacob rose early in the morning, and took the stone that he had put at his head, set it up as a pillar, and poured oil on top of it. And he called the name of that place Bethel; but the name of that city had been Luz previously (Genesis 28:10-19).

There are some very interesting insights in this passage of Scripture. Jacob knew that he had a destiny in God. He knew the promise of God that was spoken to him through His father Isaac. And yet for all that, he never walked in his destiny. As a matter of fact, he took matters into his own hands and tried to accomplish and fulfill the promise that God had for his life with his own strength and understanding. The name Jacob means, "deceiver, usurper, supplanter, and heel-catcher." Throughout his life he was found in compromising positions because of his character. He even tried to usurp God in controlling his own life and doing his "own thing" to fulfill his destiny.

In verse 11, Jacob used a stone as his pillow. This is a prophetic picture of Christ, the stone that the builder rejected as the resting place for our heads, or keeping our minds fixed upon

Him. (See Ps. 118:22, Matt. 21:42, Mark 12:10, Luke 20:17, Acts 4:11 and 1 Pet. 2:7.) It was in this posture—with his head resting on a stone—that Jacob has a revelation of Heaven and of the Lord in a "night vision," and the Lord speaks to him prophetically about his destiny.

When Jacob awakens he says a startling thing: *"How awesome is this place! This is none other than the house of God, and this is the gate of Heaven!"* (Genesis 28:17) The very first mention of the house of God in Scripture is in relation to an open Heaven.

There is a "law of first mention" regarding Scripture. When a word or passage is first used, that is the basis of our understanding of the usage of that word or the meaning of that passage throughout Scripture. Here we find that the first mention of the house of God speaks of an open Heaven, and this gives us understanding of the heart of the Father in relation to our access to Him. As temples of the Holy Spirit (see 1 Cor. 6:19), we should be living under a continuously open Heaven with free access into the heavenly realm.

From the time of this revelation through his indentured servitude to Laban, Jacob understands it is time to reconcile with his brother. Look at the prophetic picture in this passage: Even though many of us have known and understood we have a destiny in the Lord we haven't fully realized it nor have we yet entered into the fullness of our destiny. Just as Jacob walked away from his encounter with God without a noticeable change in his life, oftentimes we too walk away from an encounter with the Lord without seeing a change take place in our lives.

However, many of us are about to be released from that distant land of bondage and spiritual slavery and sent to our land of promise. See in Genesis 31:22, that Laban pursued Jacob when he discovered that he had fled...on the third day.

It took Laban seven days to finally overtake Jacob who was camped in the mountains of Gilead (see Gen. 31:23). Seven is the number of completion and perfection. It speaks of conclusion. On the seventh day there was to be a conclusion to Jacob's indentured slavery to the world system and his bondage to Laban. That system was severed once and for all. This speaks strongly to all of us that we are entering the season of release from our bondage or "servitude" to this world system.

Gilead means "the heap or mass of testimony." The testimony that we see in Laban is one of deception and lies. In Genesis 31:27, Laban speaks and says that he would have sent Jacob and his family and possessions away with a feast and blessing. Yet that was not Laban's character. He was just as much a deceiver as Jacob. Wealth and prestige were Laban's gods, and he was greedy for all the gain Jacob could bring to him. He would not have released Jacob. More than likely he would have put him to death and stolen all of his wealth.

The prophetic testimony for those of us in the Third Day and the seventh day is that the Lord is going to silence the mouths of all of our adversaries in this hour, and set us free from our slavery!

In Genesis 31:29, Laban says that it was in his power to do Jacob harm, which isn't actually the truth. God spoke to Laban and told him that he was to do no harm to Jacob, in word or deed!

In this hour we will see many people proclaim with pride and arrogance their own righteousness and power. The truth is, the Lord is dealing with them and though there is a form of obedience, the attitude of the heart has not changed.

The name *Laban* means "white; shining; gentle; brittle; to be or become white or glorious." He is the perfect example of a whitewashed tomb full of dead men's bones! Piety on the outside, but rage, self-indulgence, and self-centeredness are on the inside.

> *Woe to you, scribes and Pharisees, hypocrites! For you cleanse the outside of the cup and dish, but inside they are full of extortion and self-indulgence. Blind Pharisee, first cleanse the inside of the cup and dish, that the outside of them may be clean also. Woe to you, scribes and Pharisees, hypocrites! For you are like whitewashed tombs which indeed appear beautiful outwardly, but inside are full of dead men's bones and all uncleanness. Even so you also outwardly appear righteous to men, but inside you are full of hypocrisy and lawlessness* (Matthew 23:25-28).

There is a church right now that emulates these same characteristics. They are whitewashed on the outside, having a form of godliness, but denying the power of God! Clouds without rain! This condition will be exposed in this hour! This pseudo-spiritual church has accused those who want to press deeper into the things of God of being dangerous fanatics. They have disassociated themselves from anything that would excise the tyranny of the familiar; the decayed religious institution has them bound. They cannot stand conviction that strips bare the false veneer of their spiritual condition.

"No weapon formed against you shall prosper, and every tongue which rises against you in judgment You shall condemn. This is the heritage of the servants of the Lord, and their righteousness is from Me," Says the Lord (Isaiah 54:17).

Isaiah 54:17 is reality in this hour! On the Third Day the Lord will shut the mouths of the Labans in our lives and render the fruit of their lips ineffective! Because the motives of the heart are not right, God will shut their mouths.

Jesus said we would do the works that He did and even greater works because He went to the Father. Question: Who did the works or miracles in the Old Testament? God did them through His Word (Jesus) by the power of the Holy Spirit! Jesus did them as the Word! You see, the works that He did that we will do also encompasses what He did in the Old Testament as well as what He did in the New Testament. We are going to see every one of those same miracles again. Because we want it? No. Because God is not a man that He can lie.

If anyone teaches otherwise and does not consent to wholesome words, even the words of our Lord Jesus Christ, and to the doctrine which accords with godliness, he is proud, knowing nothing, but is obsessed with disputes and arguments over words, from which come envy, strife, reviling, evil suspicions, useless wranglings of men of corrupt minds and destitute of the truth, who suppose that godliness is a means of gain. From such withdraw yourself (1 Timothy 6:3-5).

But know this, that in the last days perilous times will come: For men will be lovers of themselves, lovers of money, boasters, proud, blasphemers, disobedient to parents, unthankful, unholy, unloving, unforgiving, slanderers, without self-control, brutal, despisers of good, traitors, headstrong, haughty, lovers of pleasure rather than lovers of God, having a form of godliness but denying its power. And from such people turn away! (2 Timothy 3:1-5).

We find the next encounter that Jacob had with the Lord as follows:

And he arose that night and took his two wives, his two female servants, and his eleven sons, and crossed over the ford of Jabbok. He took them, sent them over the brook, and sent over what he had. Then Jacob was left alone; and a Man wrestled with him until the breaking of day. Now when He saw that He did not prevail against him, He touched the socket of his hip; and the socket of Jacob's hip was out of joint as He wrestled with him. And He said, "Let Me go, for the day breaks." But he said, "I will not let You go unless You bless me!" So He said to him, "What is your name?" And he said, "Jacob." And He said, "Your name shall no longer be called Jacob, but Israel; for you have struggled with God and with men, and have prevailed." Then Jacob asked, saying, "Tell me Your name, I pray." And He said, "Why is it that you ask about My name?" And He blessed him there. And Jacob called the name of the place Peniel: "For I have seen God face to face, and my life is preserved." Just as he crossed over Penuel the sun rose on him, and he limped on his hip (Genesis 32:22-31).

Just before this passage, in Genesis 30:22-23, we see a turning point in Jacobs' life. Rachel gave birth to a son and named him Joseph. It was then when Jacob went to Laban and sought his release, and it was then he began in earnest to set his heart toward fulfilling his God-given destiny.

Jabbok means "to be emptied out; to be poured forth; to be transparently empty." It speaks of a crossing over from the self-life to the spiritual life. Here we find Jacob finally doing business with God and "wrestling" with God the entire night until the breaking of day, or the dawning of a new day. It was a new day in Jacob's life.

When this "Man" (I believe it was Jesus Himself) saw that He did not prevail against Jacob, He touched Jacob's hip and put it out of joint. He changed the way Jacob would walk from that day forward and changed his dependency from his own ability to having to rely on the Lord as his strength. We all need an encounter with the Lord which will cause us to rely completely upon Him and no longer upon our God-given abilities or strengths. Only in this way will we position ourselves to enter into our destiny.

In verse 26 we see this "Man" saying to let Him go because the day was dawning. Notice Jacob's response. He refused to let go until he received the assurance he was looking for; that his return to his country (destiny) would be successful.

On the surface, the answer given is rather strange. As a matter of fact, it wasn't an answer at all, but a question: "*What is your name?*"

The key to understanding this exchange is in understanding the Hebrew meaning of the word *name*. In every instance in the Old Testament except one, and every instance in the New

Testament, except one, the meaning of the word *name* is "character, honor, authority."

What the "Man" asked Jacob was, "what is your character?" Do you have a godly character founded in your relationship with the Lord, or do you have a worldly character based upon your relationship with the world?

What can Jacob do but be honest? He has come to the place of emptying, of being "poured forth," and he has finally become "transparently empty." Jacob is finally able to be honest not only with himself, but with God. At this point the Lord does something incredible. He responds by changing Jacob's character.

Until this point, Jacob's chief strength had been in his ability to manipulate, deceive, and supplant. In this way he was always running from Esau, Isaac, Laban, and God. Now he is limping and totally dependent upon God, and he is positioned to enter into his destiny because of an encounter with God that radically changes his character (his name).

What was his name (character) changed to? Israel. *Israel* means "Prince with God" or "to rule as God."

Here is the key: The Lord did not stop the mouth of Laban until Jacob realized he had to pursue his relationship with the Lord and make amends with his past (Esau), and so we find him at Jabbok. At that point, the Lord meets Jacob and changes his character as Jacob becomes totally dependent upon the Lord and no longer upon his own abilities or his own strength.

The question we need to ask ourselves: Are we serious about our destiny in God—serious enough to seek Him until we are changed and transformed into a man or women of Christ-like character, totally dependent upon Him for everything?

I believe there is a window of time open before us when the grace of God is being released so we can have our transforming encounter at Jabbok, and come forth as the mature sons and daughters of God we are called to be. We cannot afford to waste this opportunity.

CHAPTER FOUR

SPOILS FOR THE RIGHTEOUS

Judgment and Restored Honor

Now Dinah the daughter of Leah, whom she had borne to Jacob, went out to see the daughters of the land. And when Shechem the son of Hamor the Hivite, prince of the country, saw her, he took her and lay with her, and violated her. His soul [Strong's # 5315, appetite, lust] *was strongly attracted to Dinah the daughter of Jacob, and he loved* [Strong's # 157, a primitive root; to have affection for (sexually or otherwise)] *the young woman and spoke kindly to the young woman. So Shechem spoke to his father Hamor, saying, "Get me this young woman as a wife." And Jacob heard that he had defiled Dinah his daughter. Now his sons were with his livestock in the field; so Jacob held his peace until they came.*

Then Hamor the father of Shechem went out to Jacob to speak with him. And the sons of Jacob came in from the field when they heard it; and the men were grieved and very angry, because he had done a disgraceful thing in Israel by lying with Jacob's daughter, a thing which ought not to be done.

But Hamor spoke with them, saying, "The soul of my son Shechem longs for your daughter [the apple of your eye]. *Please give her to him as a wife. And make marriages with us; give your daughters to us, and take our daughters to yourselves. So you shall dwell with us, and the land shall be before you. Dwell and trade in it, and acquire possessions for yourselves in it." Then Shechem said to her father and her brothers, "Let me find favor in your eyes, and whatever you say to me I will give. Ask me ever so much dowry and gift, and I will give according to what you say to me; but give me the young woman as a wife."*

But the sons of Jacob answered Shechem and Hamor his father, and spoke deceitfully, because he had defiled Dinah their sister. And they said to them, "We cannot do this thing, to give our sister to one who is uncircumcised, for that would be a reproach to us. But on this condition we will consent to you: If you will become as we are, if every male of you is circumcised, then we will give our daughters to you, and we will take your daughters to us; and we will dwell with you, and we will become one people. But if you will not heed us and be circumcised, then we will take our daughter and be gone."

And their words pleased Hamor and Shechem, Hamor's son. So the young man did not delay to do the thing, because he delighted in Jacob's daughter. He was more honorable than all the household of his father. And Hamor and Shechem his son came to the gate of their city, and spoke with the men of their city, saying: "These men are at peace with us. Therefore let them dwell in the land and trade in it. For indeed the land is large enough for them. Let us take their daughters to us as wives, and let us give them our

60

daughters. Only on this condition will the men consent to dwell with us, to be one people: if every male among us is circumcised as they are circumcised. Will not their livestock, their property, and every animal of theirs be ours? Only let us consent to them, and they will dwell with us." And all who went out of the gate of his city heeded Hamor and Shechem his son; every male was circumcised, all who went out of the gate of his city. [Form of godliness without the power, see 2 Tim. 3:5] *Now it came to pass on the third day, when they were in pain, that two of the sons of Jacob, Simeon and Levi, Dinah's brothers, each took his sword and came boldly upon the city and killed all the males. And they killed Hamor and Shechem his son with the edge of the sword, and took Dinah from Shechem's house, and went out. The sons of Jacob came upon the slain, and plundered the city, because their sister had been defiled. They took their sheep, their oxen, and their donkeys, what was in the city and what was in the field, and all their wealth. All their little ones and their wives they took captive; and they plundered even all that was in the houses.*

Then Jacob said to Simeon and Levi, "You have troubled me by making me obnoxious among the inhabitants of the land, among the Canaanites and the Perizzites; and since I am few in number, they will gather themselves together against me and kill me. I shall be destroyed, my household and I." But they said, "Should he treat our sister like a harlot?" (Genesis 34:1-31).

GENESIS 34 IS THE STORY OF JACOB'S DAUGHTER, Dinah. There is a prophetic picture in this passage about the Church arising in this hour and becoming the glorious Church without spot or blemish.

The name *Dinah* means, "one who will judge." She is a type of the Church. What is it that Dinah will judge? Pride and lust—the pride of life and the lust of the eyes that lead to sin. This is what caused Shechem to take something that did not belong to him. He is a type of the world or the world system. He said that he loved the young woman, a deception that is true even today. It wasn't and isn't love, it was and is lust. And it will be judged.

The Church has been defiled and ravaged by the world system through deception and persuasion, and the world has become enmeshed within the Church. It has embraced a powerless gospel void of the character of Christ and the presence and power of God. It has been bombarded with the Hamors and Shechems of the world who demand that the Church mingle with the world and overlook the desecration of that which is called to be holy.

This onslaught of the world system into the Church has been insidious and deadly. In this story we see Shechem taking Dinah by force and defiling her through lust, and the two became one flesh. In the same way, the Church has become one flesh with the world. Now, rather than throwing off the stain and the reproach of defilement and turning to the redemptive value of the blood of Jesus, we have become entranced and comfortable in the tyranny of the familiar.

There is hope however. There was a generation that would not passively sit back and allow Shechem to defile the purity of their sister. There is a generation that is being raised up in this hour who will no longer sit by and watch the continued defiling of what the Lord had intended to be a pure holy Bride. The warriors in Jacob's household rose up and killed all of the males in the city. It took only two warriors who said, "No, we will punish the defilement of Dinah, and rescue her." They killed all the men in the city. There is a judgment coming.

Remember that throughout Scripture, God demanded that His people not mingle with those who worshiped idols. He demanded separation so that transformation could take place. The mature sons and daughters of God are grieved that the Church has been violated and ravaged—they will not tolerate it. They will rise up with the warrior spirit of Joshua and Caleb— they will take back what the enemy has stolen, plunder his goods, and demand recompense for the defilement heaped upon the Church! The wealth of the wicked is laid up for the righteous. *And the righteous shall rise in judgment against those who have defiled the Body of Christ.*

> *Do not be deceived, God is not mocked; for whatever a man sows, that he will also reap* (Galatians 6:7-8).

CHAPTER FIVE

SUDDENLY, IT WILL COME TO PASS

IMPURE HEARTS ARE SILENCED BY GOD. The righteous will rise up in judgment. But if we expect to possess God's power and His blessings, we must be mature in both faith and action. Both judgment and blessing now exist together, and the one that will possess the *wealth* of the Kingdom of God is the one whose heart conforms to the mind of Christ.

According to Strong's Concordance (OT #2428, OT #2342), *wealth* means: "chayil (khah´-yil); probably a force, whether of men, means or other resources; an army, wealth, virtue, valor, strength: KJV - able, activity, (+)army, band of men (soldiers), company, (great) forces, goods, host, might, power, riches, strength, strong, substance, train, (+)valiant (-ly), valour, virtuous (-ly), war, worthy (-ily)."

> *It came to pass after these things that the butler and the baker of the king of Egypt offended their lord, the king of Egypt. And Pharaoh was angry with his two officers, the chief butler and the chief baker. So he put them in custody in the house of the captain of the guard, in the prison, the*

place where Joseph was confined. And the captain of the guard charged Joseph with them, and he served them; so they were in custody for a while.

Then the butler and the baker of the king of Egypt, who were confined in the prison, had a dream, both of them, each man's dream in one night and each man's dream with its own interpretation. And Joseph came in to them in the morning and looked at them, and saw that they were sad. So he asked Pharaoh's officers who were with him in the custody of his lord's house, saying, "Why do you look so sad today?" And they said to him, "We each have had a dream, and there is no interpreter of it." And Joseph said to them, "Do not interpretations belong to God? Tell them to me, please."

Then the chief butler told his dream to Joseph, and said to him, "Behold, in my dream a vine was before me, and in the vine were three branches; it was as though it budded, its blossoms shot forth, and its clusters brought forth ripe grapes. Then Pharaoh's cup was in my hand; and I took the grapes and pressed them into Pharaoh's cup, and placed the cup in Pharaoh's hand."

And Joseph said to him, "This is the interpretation of it: The three branches are three days. Now within three days Pharaoh will lift up your head and restore you to your place, and you will put Pharaoh's cup in his hand according to the former manner, when you were his butler. [Blessing] *But remember me when it is well with you, and please show kindness to me; make mention of me to Pharaoh, and get me out of this house. For indeed I was stolen away from the land of the Hebrews; and also I have done nothing here that they should put me into the dungeon."*

When the chief baker saw that the interpretation was good, he said to Joseph, "I also was in my dream, and there were three white baskets on my head. In the uppermost basket there were all kinds of baked goods for Pharaoh, and the birds ate them out of the basket on my head." So Joseph answered and said, "This is the interpretation of it: The three baskets are three days. Within three days Pharaoh will lift off your head from you and hang you on a tree; and the birds will eat your flesh from you." [Judgment]

Now it came to pass on the third day, which was Pharaoh's birthday, that he made a feast for all his servants; and he lifted up the head of the chief butler and of the chief baker among his servants. Then he restored the chief butler to his butlership again, and he placed the cup in Pharaoh's hand. But he hanged the chief baker, as Joseph had interpreted to them. Yet the chief butler did not remember Joseph, but forgot him (Genesis 40:1-23).

Pay attention to the third day, *"It came to pass."* There will be a release of fulfillment— every prophetic word in your life will come to pass. *Every vision is about to break forth into the natural realm.*

"Son of man, what is this proverb that you people have about the land of Israel, which says, 'The days are prolonged, and every vision fails'? Tell them therefore, 'Thus says the Lord God: "I will lay this proverb to rest, and they shall no more use it as a proverb in Israel." But say to them, "The days are at hand, and the fulfillment of every vision. For no more shall there be any false vision or flattering

divination within the house of Israel. For I am the Lord. I speak, and the Word which I speak will come to pass; it will no more be postponed; for in your days, O rebellious house, I will say the Word and perform it," says the Lord God.'"

Again the word of the Lord came to me, saying, "Son of man, look, the house of Israel is saying, 'The vision that he sees is for many days from now, and he prophesies of times far off.' Therefore say to them, 'Thus says the Lord God: "None of My words will be postponed any more, but the word which I speak will be done," says the Lord God'" (Ezekiel 12:22-28).

This is the Third Day. The fulfillment of the Word of the Lord is no longer going to be postponed for years and years. The Word will come to pass, and it will come to pass swiftly now. You have waited for loved ones to accept Christ or the backslidden in heart to return to the Lord. You have waited for the time of maturity for your ministry. The shelf is dusty with prophetic words left for years for the time of fulfillment. The "suddenlies" of God are being released. Rejoice, for the time is now!

We must position our hearts to live in expectancy, and our expectancy should flow from a heart of gratitude as an act of worship. There will be no more delay. It is the Third Day. Speak it. Remind yourself continually of God's promises to you. Remember, on the Third Day Jesus rose from the grave, and on this Third Day your promises will be resurrected!

Understanding + Pure Heart = Power

Until the time that his [Joseph's] word came to pass, the word of the Lord tested him (Psalm 105:19).

Joseph was severely tested. His patience was refined, as all hope seemed to be lost. He was a night oracle of the Living God. The Lord would speak to him in prophetic dreams, but the words of the dreams tested him. The process with Joseph reflects the process many walk through in the fulfillment of promises. Even though the word (dream) was from the Lord, Joseph's character needed development before he could grow into the stature necessary for him to walk in that promise.

Many of us have received prophetic words, and there is an accompanying season of testing that corresponds with the fulfillment of our destiny and the word of the Lord coming to pass in our lives. The ultimate expression of the outworking of this season of testing is that we become more like Jesus in character. We must exemplify Kingdom qualities to fully walk in the promise of God for our lives, especially as it relates to the Third Day.

In the midst of testing, be encouraged; our day of release is near. The fulfillment of every promise is upon us. The fiery season of testing will come to an end as we understand the process of God at work in our lives and submit to the cleansing fire as it burns and exposes the dross in our lives.

Spiritual power is often understood more by non-Christians than Christians. If we are to be the prophetic end-time Church, the doers of "greater things," we must walk where His authority reigns. For example, people who are demonized, such as shamans (witchdoctors) and Mexican curanderos will tell you that if Christians understood that a curse without a cause cannot alight, we would be less prone to constantly blame the devil for all our shortcomings and trials. We would understand that the majority of the time what is happening in our lives is due to our own flesh and lack of understanding in regard to our inheritance in Christ. That aside, Christians who understand that a curse aimed at them will go back to the sender will be protected and walk in greater power.

> *As he loved cursing, so let it come to him. As he did not delight in blessing so let it be far from him. As he clothed himself with cursing as with his garment so let it enter his body like water and like oil into his bones. Let it be to him like the garment which covers him and for a belt with which he girds himself continually. Let this be the Lord's reward to my accusers, and to those who speak evil against my person* (Psalm 109:17-20).

It only takes once for a shaman to realize the error of his ways in trying to move against a Christian who is grounded in the truth of the Word. When they see that the Christian understands this principle, they leave them alone. Let's use a well-known minister as an example: Reinhardt Bonke.

Reinhardt Bonke was a guest of Storehouse Ministries and Impact Ministries in Seattle a few years ago. During a visit with this powerful man of God, we learned that when he visited cities in Africa, shaman would gather outside his hotel every night after the services. The ordinary people were so afraid of the shaman that they would not send them away. The shamans would light bonfires, cast curses, dance, and cut themselves in an effort to send demonic forces against Reinhardt. But he said something very important as we listened to his story: "You know, I really felt sorry for them because there is nothing that can get through the blood." He would go to bed and sleep like a baby every night. Not one of those curses ever touched him. As a matter of fact, they all went back onto the shaman. Reinhardt Bonke understands this revelation.

We all need to receive a revelation of this knowledge deep inside of us. It is the time when God says "Enemies of God, enemies of my people don't you speak either evil or good." Why? It goes back to the very first Third Day promise—He is not going to allow seeds that bring death rather than life. He told Laban not to speak good or evil because He's not going to allow those with impure motives who are of a wrong mind-set or a wrong spirit to speak even good about us because what they say is tainted.

We will begin to see the Lord silence the mouths of many in the world and in the Church in this hour as the revelation of this passage of Scripture is received by God's people. There are going to be consequences for gossips, slanderers, and backbiters—drastic consequences. This is not because the Lord doesn't love them; it is because He does. He loves all of us and His corrective discipline is redemptive.

The Lord gave me a good definition of gossip: *If we're not part of the problem or the solution, we are in gossip.* Read it again: if we're not part of the problem or the solution, we are in gossip. God deals harshly with intercessors who say, "I just want to share it because it is a prayer need." Nothing can be farther from the truth. While there may be genuine instances of this being the case, the majority of the time we are using such statements as justification to gossip about others. If we are a genuine intercessor, we pray by the Spirit, not with our understanding. We don't need to know all the details before we begin to intercede for someone. The Lord is raising the standard and calling us unto maturity. The chastening of God is about to be increased as the end of the age draws near. He will have a Church without spot or blemish. A false religious spirit will be exposed in this hour. Remember Matthew 23:25-28? We cannot afford to be whitewashed tombs!

THE PRICE OF THE PROMISE

The Spirit of God and the sword of the spirit have been released in greater measure to deal with the hidden carnal issues of our heart, and we must allow Him to examine our hearts to a greater extent than ever before. In places where revival is currently underway, the defining factor is a deep gut-wrenching repentance. People come into the presence of God and realize their wretchedness. The hidden sins we've swept under the edges of our lives are revealed in the presence of God ...we must cry out to Him for cleansing and change so we can enter into the deeper revelation He is releasing to the Church in this day.

It is an unfortunate fact that the majority of Christians today are not willing to pay the price necessary for this deeper work to take place. As I see it, there are two groups of people within the Church: forerunners and the majority.

1. Forerunners are the ones who are willing to pay the price necessary for the character of Christ to be fully developed in their lives; and,

2. The majority who must be led through to this victory by leaders who have paid the price of humility before the Lord.

The world abhors false religious trappings—we must allow these trappings to be exposed and cut from our hearts. It is sad, but true that the world has a greater capacity to discern false religious spirits than those within the Church. The world hungers for reality. Young people especially exhibit a desperate hunger for the reality of God. They come to church and many times see us play empty religious games. But when you bring them to the place of a true encounter with Jesus, then they know He is real, and their lives radically change. Truth fills them with the knowledge and power of God. Pseudo spirituality of modern day churches leaves them empty and longing for a genuine touch from a vital Christ.

> *If anyone teaches otherwise and does not consent to wholesome words, even the words of our Lord Jesus Christ and to the doctrine which accords with godliness he is proud knowing nothing, but is obsessed with disputes and arguments over words from which come envy, strife, reviling, evil suspicions, useless wranglings of men of corrupt minds and destitute of the truth who suppose that godliness is a means of gain. From such withdraw yourself* (1 Timothy 6:3-5).

Remember Laban? He had the wrong spirit, the wrong motive. Jacob was making him wealthy. It was the only thing he cared about. There are two gospels that I see being preached in the world today. There is (1) the gospel of the Kingdom—those who preach and are hungry and press into the heart and the presence of God, and (2) the gospel of mammon—those who peddle the gospel and merchandize the anointing for gain. I would like to say that this mammon-type preaching will stop immediately, but it won't. In fact, it will get worse. This sin and false representation of the gospel is going to become more and more evident as we progress further into the Third Day.

Many people, including myself, are grieved and tired of the constant quest for money in today's churches. There have been times when this spirit has manifested so strongly that I have walked out of meetings and was "dressed down" as I walked out—"How dare you grieve the Holy Spirit of God when I'm up here talking and taking an offering." That spirit is not from God.

There are those in ministry who require a minimum honorarium that must be agreed upon before that person will minister and bless the congregation. I am aware of one individual who requires a minimum of $50,000 to be a conference presenter. His terms include an expensive hotel suite—sometimes two, one for his entourage and one for himself—plus $7,000 spending money. What has the Christian church come to? What kind of example we are portraying to the world?

The saddest thing: people are so hungry for God that they are willing to pay these exorbitant fees in order to have a touch from the Lord. For $500 you can receive a prophetic word. For $1,000 right now you can receive a prophetic word and healing. That's merchandising the anointing! Whatever happened to faith?

God have mercy! The Lord will not be mocked! This "gospel" will be exposed for what it truly is because when all hell breaks loose, that gospel will not meet the need. It will become evident that it is a gospel of mammon, and it is void of power. Keep in mind that in the last days difficult times are coming, and we should be preparing for them now.

Know this, that in the last days perilous times will come. So in the last days perilous times will come for men will be lovers of themselves, lovers of money, boasters, proud, blasphemers, disobedient to parents, unthankful, unholy, unloving, unforgiving, slanderers without self-control, brutal, despisers of good, traitors, headstrong, haughty, lovers of pleasure rather than lovers of God; having a form of godliness but denying its power and from such people turn away (2 Timothy 3:1-5).

Notice the words in First Timothy 6:3 *"from such withdraw yourself,"* and Second Timothy says *"from such people turn away."* The false gospel says "well, you know, God really knows my heart. It's okay if I do these things." The truth is, God really does know your heart, and you will give an account for everything you do as well as give an account for the motives of your heart. We have deluded and deceived ourselves into thinking that God allows the call to holiness to be flexible. It is not! It is a command, not a request. The Lord is merciful if we confess our sins. However, we will reap what we sow.

Why is it in the Church that we have people who have walked with Jesus 40 or 50 years who are in the same exact spiritual condition as when they started? There is something drastically wrong with this picture. If we as a people do not press into God, learn, grow, and change from glory to glory, we are in serious trouble. Fivefold ministry carries a great responsibility in this area. These ministry offices (apostles, prophets, evangelists, pastors, teachers) found in Ephesians 4:11 are to equip the saints for the work of the ministry!

I was in Grand Forks, British Columbia, Canada, when we prayed for a woman's ear. She wanted her left ear healed, so God touched and healed her ear. I said to her, "Now there is another person here who needs prayer for their ear to be healed, you come and help me pray for them."

That dear lady said she had been saved for 40 years, and she had never, ever prayed for anyone. I almost fell over. I said, "Well, this is a good time to learn!" So she prayed for the next person, and the person was healed. Then she got excited. She had never been challenged or given the opportunity to pray for someone else throughout the entirety of her Christian experience. Today she is on fire and looking for targets of opportunity!

What is wrong with today's church? Blessed assurance, this seat is mine? Oh, what a foretaste of death on the vine? God is mobilizing the Church. There is a need for apostles, prophets, evangelists, pastors, and teachers to do what the Word says—equip the saints for the work of the ministry until all come to the unity and the maturity of the faith. Maturity and unity come through activating and releasing people into their callings instead of continually feeding them pablum to keep them in the fold—so we can reap money and be successful.

The Word says, *"from such people turn away."* There will come a time when even though we have walked with people and tried to restore them, tried to show them truth, they will refuse to change, and we will be required to walk away—not because of judgment or anger. The Lord will demand that we guard and be good stewards of what He has given us. And if those around us are not willing to walk that path, they will be removed. He will stop their mouths. A line has been drawn, and the reward of pressing into God, of knowing His heart, surpasses anything that the world could ever conceive.

His judgment is coming as swiftly as His promises to us. The visions and words of the Lord spoken over your life and over the Church as a whole, will come to pass suddenly, in the blink of an eye. The promises of God will enter the natural realm. The judgment of God will enter the natural realm. So how do we prepare?

CHAPTER SIX

PREPARATION FOR GLORY

Then the Lord said to Moses, "Go to the people and conse-crate them today and tomorrow and let them wash their clothes. And let them be ready for the third day..." (Exodus 19:10-11)

PREPARATION

THE CONSECRATION AND SANCTIFICATION OF THE CHURCH is meant to set us apart from the world. The last two thousand years, the last "two days," God has worked in us to prepare us for this Third Day. "*...For on the third day the Lord will come down upon Mount Sinai in the sight of all of His people*" (Exod. 19:11). The Lord is going to come down on the Church in the sight of all of His people on the Third Day. The longing of our hearts, the passionate pursuit, and the hunger for the deeper things of God has been released on the Church. Preparation for the Third Day requires stewardship of that passion and perseverance in the pursuit of the hidden secrets of the Lord. Consecration and separation is our command. God's response is His manifest presence. It will leave us without words, and on our faces before the Living God.

> *Let them be ready for the third day, for on the third day the Lord will come down upon Mount Sinai in the sight of all the people. You shall set bounds for the people all around saying, 'Take heed to yourselves that you do not go up on the mountain or touch its base.' Whoever touches the mountain shall surely be put to death. Not a hand shall touch him but he shall surely be stoned or shot with an arrow; whether man or beast, he shall not live. When the trumpet sounds long they shall come near the mountain* (Exodus 19:11-13).

Be aware that in this time, God will not share His glory with anyone! For years people have come to me after a meeting and said, "Oh that was so good. Thank you!" My reply is always, "It wasn't me; it was God." And as amazing as it seems, people will argue with me. But I have learned through experience that the glory belongs to God. I tried to take the credit once…and paid dearly for more than a year. The Lord said to me, "If you ever, ever take credit or touch my glory again, I will not allow you to stand before my people again!" Flesh will not be permitted into the presence of His glory.

The Lord is beginning to move in unprecedented ways by His Spirit, and no one will take His glory as if by their own merits and wisdom they had attained to an exalted state of spiritual maturity. There will be no spiritual superstars. It will not be about Steve Stunning Evangelist or Prophet Profound. God will sovereignly break into our reality, and there will be no arguments as His Spirit takes control and does what He pleases. The Body of Christ will be corporately mobilized and released. The harvest must be won. When the trumpet sounds, and the voices of the prophets speak loudly, come near the mountain.

EARLY MORNING, THIRD DAY

Where are we in God's timetable? I believe we are currently living during the early morning on the Third Day.

> *Then it came to pass on the third day, in the morning, that there were thunderings and lightnings and a thick cloud on the mountain and the sound of the trumpet was very loud so that all the people that were in the camp trembled. And Moses brought the people out of the camp to meet with God and they stood at the foot of the mountain. Now* [the church] *Mount Sinai was completely in smoke* [the glory] *because the Lord descended upon it in fire. Its smoke ascended like the smoke of the furnace and the whole mountain quaked greatly. And when the blast of the trumpet sounded long and became louder and louder, Moses spoke and God answered him by voice. Then the Lord came down upon Mount Sinai on the top of the mountain...* (Exodus 19:16-20).

Catch this sequence: the glory came down, the fire came down, the earth began to quake, and then God came down. Some of us have tasted the glory. Some have tasted the fire. Very few of us have tasted the quaking (the fear of the Lord). Have you been watching the signs? God is about to step down from Heaven to earth. You will begin to hear shortly about outbreaks of glory, fire, and quaking before the Lord. Wherever you are, ask yourself, why not here? Why not now? What does it take to be a partaker of the move of God?

We must consecrate ourselves to be ready for this Third Day. Jesus said: "*Be ye holy, even as I am holy.*" The prerequisite for being a priest was holiness. God is holy, therefore the priest must be holy. That command has not changed. We must have a deep revelation of His holy nature, and then we must become holy as He commanded. He does not ask us to do something we cannot do. He equips us with the ability or gives us the grace to accomplish His will on the earth. We must set ourselves apart unto God through prayer, fasting, reading, and meditating in His Word, and fellowshipping with one another in love.

Again, look at the sequence of the Third Day. Watch what you say. Love the God of the promise more than the promise of God. The impure heart will not speak about you either good or bad. Sons and daughters will rise in judgment against those who have defiled and violated the Lord's Church. The prophetic promises that God has given you will now become reality. They will come to pass suddenly. The glory of God will transform the Church! The whole earth will be filled with the knowledge of the glory of God because God's people will demonstrate His glory.

Peter had a touch of God's glory when his own shadow fell on people, and they were healed. We will see that again. The sick and broken will touch you because of the virtue of God that flows out of you, and they will be healed. Why? Because God's glory is being released, and we will be clothed in it. There is a difference between anointing and glory.

A friend of mine, Dr. Flo Ellers, described the difference this way: "Anointing gives you an enabling beyond what you ever had before but the glory causes you to fall on your face before God. In glory, you do nothing." You see, it will be all of Him, and there will be nothing of our carnal nature able to stand! The day of His glory has arrived.

CHAPTER SEVEN

PURIFICATION

Intimacy to Reflect the King

The remainder of the flesh of the sacrifice on the third day must be burned with fire (Leviticus 7:17).

ON THIS THIRD DAY, we must find the revelation of the crucified life, build an altar before God, and come to Him in the secret place where all sin is divested. Scripture speaks of secret sins, those that have taken up residence in us...sins of which we are often unaware. It is always easy to point to other people's faults, while we ourselves are blind to our own spiritual condition. But on this Third Day, the remainder of our flesh must be recognized and dealt with. He demands a Church without spot or wrinkle. That means He must have precedence over our desires and feelings. We have to determine in our hearts that obedience to God is better than sacrifice. His Word is our command. *We must find the place where His desire, His command, becomes our passion.*

There were multitudes that followed Jesus. On the day of Pentecost, 120 were in the upper room, yet 500 had seen Him after He had risen from the dead. He told them all to tarry—but only 120 did. He sent 70 out to do the works of the Holy Spirit, but He took only 12 men aside to explain the parables to them. It is during that intimate time with Jesus when revelation and knowledge are given.

From this group of 12, only three would have a special time together with Him, including when they were on the Mount of Transfiguration. Yet there was only one, John the Beloved, who leaned upon the breast of Jesus, and knew His very heartbeat. For years I said "Lord, I want to be that one—and if your heartbeat even has a murmur in it of longing or desire, that will be my command. That will become my passion."

One day the Holy Spirit said to me, "You know something, Bruce, you can be closer than that." I said, "How?" He said, "You can be in Me." I never realized the truth of that statement, but the Bible says, "*…it is no longer I who live, but Christ lives in me; and the life which I now live in the flesh, I live by the faith of the Son of God…*" (Gal. 2:20). And John 14:20 says, *"At that day you will know that I am in my Father, and you in Me, and I in you."*

We must live, not in our weak faith, but in His supernatural faith. We must understand as Paul did, it's got to be all of Him, and none of me. John the Baptist said in John 3:30, *"He must increase, but I must decrease."* Jesus is calling us to crucify our flesh and to take up our cross daily and follow Him, and it must be an act of our will.

Ask the Holy Spirit, "I know there are issues in my flesh that need to be dealt with, would you please slowly begin to show me these things so I can deal with them?" If He showed them to us quickly, we would despair of life. But in His gracious timing, He will show us and expose things in our lives that are displeasing to

Him. It is this deeper work that we need to have completed in our lives. The blatant, fleshy things are obvious to all. But the secret, hidden things are the "little foxes that spoil the vine." (Song of Sol. 2:15). All of us have them. As we determine, in Christ, to allow the Spirit of God to deal with us, a transformation will begin to take place, and the Lord will become pre-eminent in our lives.

> *The refining pot is for silver and the furnace for gold, and a man is valued by what others say of him* (Proverbs 27:21).

The fruit of your life speaks louder than the words that you use to proclaim your own righteousness. The refining pot is for silver. Silver speaks of sanctification and redemption. It is the place to *"work out your own salvation with fear and trembling"* (Phil. 2:12). It is a life-long journey. Unfortunately, in our Western world with our instant gratification mind-set, we expect instant spiritual maturity without the corresponding process of working out our own salvation with fear and trembling. The message of the gospel is one of a crucible, the place where change is wrought by allowing the God of Heaven to remove our impurities in the refining pot of redemption.

CHRIST-LIKE CHARACTER

"The furnace is for gold." The remainder of the flesh must be burned with fire. The furnace of affliction is where the fire melts us and makes us fit to pour into God's plan for us. He skims off the dross, and we come forth as pure gold, a vessel of honor, without spot or wrinkle. Gold speaks of purity and holiness. It is the call of God today.

We are faced with a challenge: we must rethink the time of testing and trial. The furnace is actually a place of reward. Shadrach, Meshach, and Abed-Nego received their reward when they refused to bow their knee and worship an idol of the king. Most think the furnace was the test. No, that was their reward for obedience to God. When they went into the furnace, they met the Lord—Face to face. We have conditioned ourselves to flee wilderness experiences and the furnace of affliction because we do not like to be uncomfortable, and we fear the process of "becoming." But the furnace is the very place for a Face-to-face encounter with the Living God!

As you study the Gospels, you will find that Jesus retreated into a wilderness place to be alone with God on a consistent basis. Yet we run from the wilderness experience. We have misconstrued the purpose of the wilderness experience and relegated it to a time of pain, turmoil, and defeat. Jesus, however, says the opposite. He knew that the wilderness was a place of preparation and communion with the Father that would prepare Him for the next encounter with the masses. And He came forth renewed in the power and the anointing of the Holy Ghost. The wilderness was a place of purification and preparation. He consistently embraced and looked forward to each encounter with God there.

We will have wilderness experiences consistently throughout our lives. What are we going to do with them? Will we lament, cry, and whine? Or, will we recognize these times as an opportunity to be alone with God as He prepares us for our next assignment through study, prayer, and fasting as the Lord changes us and further conforms us into the image of His Son? There are no distractions in the wilderness save one—our flesh.

People do not want to be around us when we're in the wilderness because they see it as a time of punishment. No, it is a time of opportunity that we may have missed. I used to think Paul was mentally imbalanced when he wrote, "We glory in tribulations." (see Rom. 5:3). I thought that maybe one of those 40-pound rocks hit him in the head. It made no sense to me until the tests and trials of my own life helped me understand the process.

As we yield ourselves to God during trials, Christ-like character comes forth. Although I don't volunteer for tests and trials, I don't dread those times of testing and trial as much as I once did. I know if there is a wilderness experience ahead of me, it is because the Lord is about to do something in me.

I beseech you therefore, brethren, by the mercies of God, that you present your bodies a living sacrifice, holy, acceptable to God, which is your reasonable service. And do not be conformed to this world, but be transformed by the renewing of your mind, that you may prove what is that good and acceptable and perfect will of God (Romans 12:1-2).

Present your bodies a living sacrifice—what does that mean? We must take this fleshly life, our worldly thoughts and attitudes, and willingly place them upon the altar of sacrifice and say, "Father, we need to be refined with fire."

The next great move of God will be an outpouring of fire. It will consume all that is of the flesh and in turn deposit holiness and the fear of God within us. The Lord will have the reverence, honor, and respect due Him. This next move of God will absolutely level the playing field. All of the evil we have spoken about each other will be destroyed. The fear of God will constrain us, and put a guard on our lips. It will keep us in the place where we would rather die than grieve His Spirit. The fear of God in our lives allows us to be positioned for the presence of God to enter our homes, our churches, and our communities. We stand on the verge of a revelation of the fear of God that will grip whole church communities...and God will say, "*Do not touch My anointed ones, And do My prophets no harm*" (Ps. 105:15 NASB).

THE FEAR OF ALMIGHTY GOD

Here is an example from the life of my dad's Russian friend. The incident occurred in Russia during the cold war, during the time of the Iron Curtain. The man was arrested for his faith in Jesus. He refused to renounce the Lord, so he spent 25 years in prison where, on a daily basis, he would be beaten mercilessly. They put his feet in stocks and beat them to a pulp. To this day, he can barely walk because his feet have severe nerve damage. A light bulb was turned on in his cell 24 hours a day in an attempt to deprive him of sleep. If he started to fall asleep, they would throw water on him or slap him until he was almost comatose with exhaustion. Every few weeks for 25 years, they would drag him into the interrogation room to coerce him into renouncing Christ. But he refused to break and renounce Jesus—and he continued to lead his fellow prisoners to Christ.

One day, the captain of the guard hauled his broken, bloody body to the interrogation room and tied him to the chair. In his heart this man cried out to the Lord and said, "God, I don't think I can take any more, I'm at my end!" The Lord spoke softly to his spirit and said, "Give that captain a word from Me." So he said to the captain, "I have a word for you from God."

The atheist guard mocked him and replied with a sarcastic laugh, "Oh yeah, what's that?" The prisoner replied, "Touch not my anointed and do my prophet no harm." The statement infuriated the guard. He drew his clenched fist back to strike the prisoner, and fell over dead of a massive heart attack at 39 years of age. The other guards carted his body out of the room.

The prisoner waited there for a few hours, and a lieutenant came in. He was going to take over where the captain had left off. The prisoner turned to the lieutenant and said, "I've got a word for you from God." The lieutenant angrily replied, "Yeah, what's that?" Again the prisoner spoke the words, "Touch not my anointed and do my prophet no harm." The lieutenant also mocked him, replied in a sarcastic tone, and began to blaspheme the Lord. As the lieutenant was drawing back to strike him, he fell over dead of a massive heart attack at age 28.

The next guard came in and warned everyone present, "Don't touch that man because his God will kill you." They untied the prisoner and returned him to his cell. From that day forward no one touched or abused him.

He paid a price. He endured as much as he could. His flesh was burned on the altar of sacrifice. We, too, must pay the price required of us. We can choose to take the remainder of our flesh on the Third Day, and put it on the altar of sacrifice, and be prepared in the hour of His visitation. When the glory of God comes upon you and the fear of God grips you, no one will be able to abuse you.

The hour is near. We don't have years and years to practice and prepare before God begins to pour out His Spirit. Behold, He comes quickly. What are we doing to get ready?

BE CLEAN

Look closely at Numbers chapter 19 regarding the laws of purification:

> *He who touches the dead body of anyone shall be unclean seven days. He shall purify himself with the water on the third day and on the seventh day;* [Remember, we live in both the third and seventh days.] *then he will be clean. But if he does not purify himself on the third day and on the seventh day, he will not be clean* (Numbers 19:11-12).

We have an unction from the Spirit of God. Verse 11 says anyone who touches the dead body of anyone shall be unclean. Let me paint a different picture for you. Ezekiel 38 talks about the valley of dry bones—think of them as the covenant people of God. Many of the churches throughout the world preach a "gospel of ease." The messages have become seeker sensitive and user friendly. This practice is a stench in the nostrils of God. They preach a form of godliness while denying the power of God. This is the way of death and decay. However, the time of visitation has come and once we have tasted what God is doing the people will not turn back to a dead and lifeless religious experience. The Word is clear about separating ourselves from a brother or sister who call themselves by the name of Jesus but continue in sin and refuse to change.

Many also have a misconstrued understanding of the Scriptures regarding sinners. We somehow think it is pious and holy to love and accept them with their sin—rather than to love and help them out of their sinful life. The Lord never said to love sinners and accept their sin. He did say to love the sinner and hate the sin.

If we understand that we are to crucify our flesh (see Lev. 7:17), from that point we are going to walk by the Spirit of God…and the Spirit of God is love. Whether that love is strong or gentle, it is still love. That which is holy cannot mingle with that which is unholy. I'm not talking about the sinners in the world—we're called to go into their midst and win them to Jesus. I'm talking about those in the church who refuse to accept what God is saying and doing. Many have refused already, and the glory has departed. How do we respond to them? We pray and intercede for them just as Jesus, our High Priest, prays and intercedes for us. We lay down our lives that they can know the truth.

The Lord is calling us on the Third Day and the seventh day to wash even our clothes.

> *The clean person shall sprinkle the unclean on the third day and on the seventh day, and on the seventh day he shall purify himself, wash his clothes, and bathe in water; and at evening he shall be clean* (Numbers 19:19).

> *Husbands, love your wives, just as Christ also loved the church and gave Himself for her, that He might sanctify and cleanse her with the washing of water by the Word* (Ephesians 5:25-26).

Sanctification and cleansing comes into our life by the washing of the water of the Word. The best times you will ever have with God, the times when God forms your character to a greater extent, are *always* the intimate, alone times with God. We are called to be stones, living stones, that fit into the temple of God. We are part of the whole. But a stone must be chiseled, pounded, broken, and formed in order to rightly fit into the whole of the temple. This occurs as we spend time in the Word and in our alone times with the Lord in prayer, praise, and waiting on Him. Christianity is not a Sunday spectator sport. The "Sunday only" mentality produces a crippled and weak individual.

Victory for us exists in the life of Christ that is formed in us. Victory comes through strategies that are imparted directly to us by God in and through His Word. Victory comes through supernatural revelation imparted directly from the throne of God. None of these occur without spending more than just our cursory duty on Sunday morning going to our local church. Because the biblical mandate is to purify ourselves and to be clean on this Third Day, we need to determine within ourselves to spend as much time with the Lord as we can in our pursuit of Christ-like character.

On this Third Day, we are to be sanctified and set apart; consecrated for the use of the Master in this final hour. There is no more time to go through the motions of playing church. It is time to become the living, vibrant Church. The greatest anointing that we will witness will be demonstrated outside the walls of the local church.

I believe that shortly we will be seeing spontaneous meetings in Wal-Mart, your local Starbucks, and Costco—wherever believers find themselves. The Spirit of God is moving to such an extent that everywhere you go you will hear the name of Jesus on the lips of someone who is hungry. Even the unsaved will notice that something has changed in the spiritual atmosphere of your community or city.

REFLECTED GLORY

And do this, knowing the time, that now it is high time to awake out of sleep; for now our salvation is nearer than when we first believed. The night is far spent, the day is at hand. Therefore let us cast off the works of darkness, and let us put on the armor of light (Romans 13:11-12).

It is an imperative that we understand and obey this Scripture and *"put on the armor of light."* We know that *"God is light, and in Him there is no darkness."* (1 John 1:5). When was the last time you had to put on sunglasses because the person next to you was radiating and reflecting the glory of God? We are called to reflect God's glory. An important spiritual principle to understand: that which you behold, you become; and that which has your attention, you empower.

When you look at the Son, you will reflect the Son. *When your heart, your passion, your pursuit, everything about you is focused on Him, you cannot help but reflect Jesus.* We need to become seekers, willing to search for truth. People who seek for truth will find Him. As the world grows darker and darker, the Lord and His people will shine brighter and brighter. The glory of the Lord has risen upon you. (See Isaiah 60:1.) He has risen upon you because He has anointed you to do something for His glory.

> *Let us walk properly, as in the day, not in revelry and drunkenness, not in lewdness and lust, not in strife and envy. But put on the Lord Jesus Christ, and make no provision for the flesh, to fulfill its lusts* (Romans 13:13).

Paul in Corinthians says, "I can't give you meat. You're in need of milk. Where there is envy and strife and bickering and wrangling and all these things among you, aren't you still in need of milk and not yet able to consume meat?" (See Hebrew 5:12.)

What is the meat of the Word? Is it love? Yet love is not the meat of the Word if we don't live it. Faith is not the meat of the

Word if we don't walk in it. Meat exists when the people of God put into practice the truth of the Word, and it is developed until fruit comes forth. We will never be positioned to receive meat until we adhere to the admonition of making no provision for our flesh. When we live the crucified life we are fulfilling Romans 13:13.

> *Therefore, my beloved, as you have always obeyed, not as in my presence only, but now much more in my absence, work out your own salvation with fear and trembling* (Philippians 2:12).

Fear of what? Fear of God! We must work out our salvation. But you say, "Wait a minute, I'm saved. What's to work out?" You overcome by the blood of the Lamb and the word of your testimony, and confession is made unto salvation. We've got to work on our salvation. We have to line up with the Word of God and do what the Word of God says. That's working out our salvation. We have to allow the character of Christ to be formed in us. Let me reiterate, this is a life-long process, and it takes a determination on our part to persevere in this endeavor. The good news is, the longer we pursue the Lord in anticipation of becoming wholly sanctified, the easier the journey becomes as little by little, each day, we are changed from glory to glory.

The "tyranny of the familiar" grips us all. We've become used to certain things in our lives, and we are loath to let them go because we get comfortable in the rhythms and patterns of our daily life, even though what we are doing may be wrong or harmful. That's the tyranny of the familiar—it is bondage whether we recognize it as such or not.

We cannot justify ourselves and make excuses any longer. It is time for us to purify ourselves and build an altar to burn (crucify) the remainder of the flesh of our sacrifice. We are a living sacrifice, and we need to place ourselves on that altar. We must continually purify ourselves with the washing of the water of the Word. As we determine in our hearts to adjust our lives and our thinking to what He has spoken in His Word, we will find ourselves prepared and fit for the Master's use in this hour.

CHAPTER EIGHT

THIRD DAY STRATEGIES

New Ideas from the Throne of God

And it came to pass when all the kings who were on this side of the Jordan, in the hills and in the lowland and in all the coasts of the Great Sea toward Lebanon—the Hittite, the Amorite, the Canaanite, the Perizzite, the Hivite, and the Jebusite—heard about it, that they gathered together to fight with Joshua and Israel with one accord (Joshua 9:1-2).

THE WORD *JORDAN* MEANS "to descend" or literally, "to go downward." Figuratively, it speaks of entering the Promised Land, or the new life in Christ. There is a battle to be fought and won in the Promised Land. It is not so much an end in and of itself, but a place of deeper revelation and intimacy with the Lord, a place that must be contended for. As we do so, we will find rich rewards for our consistent reliance upon the Lord for His strategies of entering into our promised land. You will notice that the only time the Israelites were defeated is when they failed to inquire of God for a strategy. When they chose to do something on their own, with their own understanding and their own strength, they were defeated.

When we try to figure things out on our own and when we try to accomplish the will of God by the arm of flesh, we will always end up in defeat rather than victory. We have a tendency to make a mess of our lives because we do not inquire of Him, and then we blame the Lord for where we find ourselves.

But when the inhabitants of Gibeon heard what Joshua had done to Jericho and Ai, they worked craftily, and went and pretended to be ambassadors. And they took old sacks on their donkeys, old wineskins torn and mended, old and patched sandals on their feet, and old garments on them-selves; and all the bread of their provision was dry and moldy. And they went to Joshua, to the camp at Gilgal, and said to him and to the men of Israel, "We have come from a far country; now therefore, make a covenant with us." Then the men of Israel said to the Hivites, "Perhaps you dwell among us; so how can we make a covenant with you?" But they said to Joshua, "We are your servants." And Joshua said to them, "Who are you, and where do you come from?" So they said to him: "From a very far country your servants have come, because of the name of the Lord your God; for we have heard of His fame and all that He did in Egypt, and all that He did to the two kings of the Amorites who were beyond the Jordan—to Sihon king of Heshbom, and Og king of Bashan, who was at Ashtaroth. Therefore our eld-ers and all the inhabitants of our country spoke to us, say-ing, 'Take provisions with you for the journey, and go to meet them, and say to them "We are your servants; now therefore, make a covenant with us."' This bread of ours we took hot for our provision from our houses on the day we departed to come to you. But now look, it is dry and moldy. And these wineskins which we filled were new, and see, they are torn; and these our garments and our sandals have become old because of the very long journey." Then the men of Israel took some of their provisions; **but they did not ask counsel of the Lord.** *So Joshua made peace with them, and made a covenant with them to let them live; and the rulers of the congregation swore to them* (Joshua 9:3-15).

How often have we in the Church made covenant with the world because of human compassion without godly wisdom? We enable behaviors in people because of our unsanctified human compassion when there is no godly wisdom and leading. In doing so, we have made covenant with the works of darkness, with behaviors that are sinful in the eyes of God, all because we do not inquire of the Lord.

My dad and I used to discuss Matthew 5:42, that we are to give to those who ask, asking nothing in return. This is right in the sight of God, however, when you begin to cause people to be dependent upon you because of laziness on their part or through manipulation, you feed sin and not need. We "make covenant" with behaviors that are contrary to the Word of God and His very nature because we did not inquire of Him for a strategy and for the wisdom about how to implement His plan. Joshua and the people of God did not ask His counsel (see Joshua 9).

We had a banner hanging in our training center in Lynnwood, Washington, that proclaimed, "Ask God." Asking questions of those around you is a good practice, but we need to make God the first person we turn to for answers. Before we make a decision or do anything, we must go to the Word of God and the God of the Word in prayer.

In that training center, after four or five years of seeing that sign and applying the principle, the transformation that took place in the lives of the people was amazing. That is why we teach when praying for individuals: Don't just lay hands on them and start praying. Inquire of the Lord what He is saying and doing in that particular situation. Take the time to assess from a heavenly perspective what is happening in each situation.

A simple example. Say a person asked for prayer. I would inquire about the need.

"Well, my shin is black and blue and it really hurts."

Most well-meaning Christians would immediately pray for the symptom. However, if you take the time to step back and ask the Lord what is happening in this situation, you may just receive an answer similar to this:

"The problem isn't the bruised shin. He's got an anger problem. He got angry at his dog, kicked at the animal and missed, hitting his shin against the chair."

Now we know how to focus our prayer so that the root issue is resolved and from that point on he won't have a problem with bruised and swollen shins!

We must face the true issue and deal with it so the next time that person comes to a service, he cannot say that the prayer didn't work. Symptoms are not the issue—the underlying cause is what we need to pray about. We are to set the captives free by dealing with the true issues and in doing so providing total healing through Jesus Christ.

And it happened at the end of three days, after they had made a covenant with them, that they heard that they were their neighbors who dwelt near them (Joshua 9:16).

The Lord specifically said not to make a covenant with anybody in this Promised Land. And we're not to make covenant with anybody in our promised land either. Our promised land is not only a spiritual place, but a natural place—it is the world. The Lord said we are to have dominion over it and everything that lives in it (see Gen. 1:28). We cannot do this by becoming entangled and enmeshed in the world. If we are friends with the world, we are enemies of God.

Then the children of Israel journeyed and came to their cities on the third day. Now their cities were Gibeon, Cephirah, Beeroth, and Kirjath Jearim. But the children of Israel did not attack them, because the rulers of the congregation had sworn to them by the Lord God of Israel. And all the congregation complained against the rulers. Then all the rulers said to all the congregation, "We have sworn to them by the Lord God of Israel; now therefore, we may not touch them. This we will do to them: We will let them live, lest wrath be upon us because of the oath which we swore to them." And the rulers said to them, "Let them live, but let them be woodcutters and water carriers for all the congregation, as the rulers had promised them." Then Joshua called for them, and he spoke to them, saying, "Why have you deceived us, saying 'We are very far from you, when you dwell near us? Now therefore, you are cursed and none of you shall be freed from being slaves—woodcutters and water carriers for the house of my God.'" So they answered Joshua and said, "Because your servants were clearly told that the Lord your God commanded His servant Moses to give you all the land, and to destroy all the inhabitants of the land from before you; therefore we were very much afraid for our lives because of you, and have done this thing" (Joshua 9:17-24).

Thank God, He will redeem our foolishness. The fear of God caused these people to deceive the Israelites. And the Israelites lacked wisdom and discernment. So they entered into covenant contrary to the will of God—yet they were constrained to keep their vow because the character of God would not allow them to do anything else. Some of us have made vows with the enemies of the Cross. God says that you made the covenant, but I will turn this and cause them to become your slaves.

The world is about to give up its wealth. They have tried to thwart the move of God because they are by nature contrary to the Spirit of God. The woodcutters and the watering gate were to be used for the temple of God. Transference of the wealth is taking place within the Kingdom of God, as well as the wealth of the wicked coming into the Kingdom. There have been those in the Kingdom of God who have hoarded the wealth for themselves and filled up their barns and silos, instead of distributing the wealth to those who have labored long and hard for God with no return. The Lord is about to supernaturally level the playing field. Some will need a Joseph figure in their lives because they squander money due to a lack of maturity; however, there is a redistribution about to take place.

God will expose the things in our lives that we have kept close to us, believing they were fine. We must lose the "Madison Avenue Marketing" techniques used in church growth. The time for figuring things out on our own is long past. The Word says you are foolish when you compare yourselves among yourselves and try to emulate each other. (2 Cor. 10:12) There is a strong difference between building the house on your own, and asking counsel of God. There is a pastor we know of who tried every new church growth technique—from seminars and books, to all the latest trends. His church went from 250 members down to about 30. He tried everything worldly and "killed" his church because he modeled it after man's ideas instead of God's wisdom.

In this Third Day, we must not make covenant with man's mentality or man's terms of growth for God's Kingdom. It will no longer be allowed. All pastors need to fast and pray to seek the Lord's strategy for His Church, then we will all find good success.

Joshua 9:16 speaks of the deception that entraps us as we enter into covenant with the world through the pride of seeking our own council rather than inquiring of the Lord. The people of Israel made a covenant with liars. They were told a lie and because they did not inquire of the Lord they had to keep their word with the lie. We must remove ourselves from the traditions of men that run contrary to the Word of God and separate ourselves from those who through deceit cause us to make covenant with the world.

Jesus Himself chastised the Pharisees for thwarting the key of knowledge (see Luke 11:52) with the traditions of men and refusing to allow the people to receive what God had for them. If you want to enter into the promised land of this Third Day, you must seek the Lord for His strategies in every facet of your life.

DIVINE INHERITANCE

The fulfillment of the promise of the Third Day is found in Joshua 9:17: "*Then the children of Israel journeyed and came to their cities on the third day...*"

After the Lord deals with our sins, heart issues, and our covenants with the world, we will enter the inheritance He promised. Each tribe had its own city and own plot of ground that was given to them. You and I on this Third Day will also enter into that inheritance. For so long we have been saying, "Well, that is already ours. We've already been walking in it." No, we haven't. We have been on a journey toward it. We have to battle the enemies of the Cross and the sin in the flesh until we can get to the place where we have matured enough to receive the inheritance.

Remember, adoption in the Near Eastern culture is different than adoption in Western countries. There, a child was born into the family and when that child came of age, mature enough to help in the family estate, then the child was adopted as a joint heir by the parents. Although he was born into the family, he was adopted when he was mature enough to work in the estate and the affairs of the family.

That's the place we're coming to on the Third Day. We're growing up into Him—so that we can be the adopted sons and daughters of God. He speaks of Son-ship and heir-ship and full maturity. This will be the time when we move from being in position to *inherit* the promises to *possessing* these same promises as mature sons and daughters of God.

We have not possessed them yet. We've confessed them; we've struggled to grow up enough to try to walk in them. But it is time to enter the inheritance and move into the fullness of the Lord for our lives: *maturity*.

The Lord has amazing promises for us! If you study the names of the cities promised to the people of Israel, you will see His promises for us. Each person is given unique spiritual DNA.

Each person is separate, with unique messages, unique understanding, and a unique place in God, and this in turn makes up the whole.

Daniel's prophetic life was unique as was Jeremiah's and Elijah's, yet they stand as part of the whole. Each of us is different according to our spiritual DNA, yet all of our messages become part of the overall plan of God. Each different revelation, each different view and insight brings the full overall picture.

We are about to enter into the inheritance that is suitable to the calling and function that God gave us in His Body. We will walk in victory in this Third Day because we have dealt with the remainder of the flesh, we have purified ourselves, and we have begun to wash others to help them into a place of purity and holiness. The things we did in ignorance because we did not consult with Him will be removed, and we will enter our inheritance.

Imagine that you visit a town, or walk into a church, and everyone in the city falls on their face before God in tearful repentance. The same experiences that marked the lives of saints such as Smith Wigglesworth and Charles Finney, are ours by inheritance. The light of the glory of God is upon you—it can and will be seen. Factories can shut down, and bars close; prostitutes and drug addicts will be healed, delivered, and set free. This is your inheritance—all of the treasures of darkness: a lost and dying world.

In First Samuel 7:2-3, the ark remained in Eleazar's house for 20 years. Eleazar prospered in everything he did because the manifest presence of God was there. That is our inheritance. The veil was torn, and we now have free access into the throne room of God. The presence of God in our lives is our inheritance. As we contend for the fulfillment of our inheritance on this Third Day, everything we do will prosper, and we will mature into the possession of the inheritance of God's presence.

> *Now it happened when David and his men came to Ziklag, on the third day, that the Amalekites had invaded the south and Ziklag, attacked Ziklag and burned it with fire, and had taken captive the women and those who were there, from small to great; they did not kill anyone, but carried them away and went on their way. So David and his men came to the city and there it was burned with fire; and their wives, their sons, their daughters had been taken captive.* [Backslidden into the world and were ensnared]. *Then David and the people who were with him lifted up their voices and wept until they had no more power to weep* (1 Samuel 30:1-4).

Grief is a natural process, but after grief comes anger. First Samuel 30:5 says that two of David's wives were among the captives, and David was greatly distressed. That means his grief was beyond measure; it was more than he could bear. Not only had his wives been captured and his possessions stolen, but key people spoke of stoning him. The souls of all the people were grieved over the loss of their own sons and daughters. It began with grief; it turned to anger.

Does this sound familiar? When things go wrong in our lives we look for someone to blame, or stone—so let's stone the pastor. That's how we shed innocent blood with our mouth—we stone people with our words and actions. We curse them because we are angry in our circumstances and need someone to blame.

...But David strengthened himself in the Lord his God (1 Samuel 30:6).

This was a man after God's own heart. Sin or great victory, despair or joy, he always sought God the Father. It didn't matter where he found himself; his first inclination was to turn to God. His heart was toward God even when he was greatly distressed and cried until he had no strength. He comforted himself in the Lord. He strengthened himself in the Lord. He didn't just comfort himself; he strengthened himself for the task ahead. Strength comes from intimacy with God. Strength for another day or maybe strength for the next ten minutes is all we can muster. But it is strength to go on. We need to make the Lord our strength. We need to make Him our strong right hand. We need to turn to Him for comfort in everything.

Then David said to Abiathar the priest, Ahimelech's son, "Please bring the ephod here to me." And Abiathar brought the ephod to David so David inquired of the Lord... (1 Samuel 30:7-8).

The ephod literally speaks of the high priest's shoulder piece. It was the signet that gave the priest the right to go into the temple, to worship God and intercede on behalf of the people. That's what David meant when he asked for the ephod—I need that mantle so that I can go in and intercede and receive a strategy from God.

David's actions were not only amazing, but quite telling. He had been serving and honoring the Lord and was pleasing to the Lord in all that he did. Suddenly, on a day like any other day, all he loved and worked for was lost. Rather than shake his fist at God and succumb to depression and bitterness, he turned to the

Lord and strengthened himself in God. When he found the strength he needed to continue, he inquired of God asking for a strategy. Even when those who were closest to him, his very own men, were breathing threats against him, he turned to the Lord.

> … *"Shall I pursue this troop? Shall I overtake them?" And He answered him, "Pursue, for you shall surely overtake them and without fail recover all"* (1 Samuel 30:8).

On the Third Day, without fail, as you seek the Lord for His strategies you will recover everything the enemy has stolen from you! That's the Word of the Lord to us! As we strengthen ourselves in the Lord and inquire of God for a strategy, without fail, we will pursue and overtake the devil and command him to give back everything he has stolen. We are going to get it back, without fail.

RESTORATION

> *So David went, he and six hundred men who were with him and came to the Brook Besor where those stayed who were left behind. But David pursued, he and four hundred men; for two hundred stayed behind who were so weary they could not cross the Brook Besor* (1 Samuel 30:9-10).

Besor is an interesting word. It is a primitive root meaning "to bear, to bring, to carry, to preach, to tell good things or tidings." These weary warriors were standing in the place of good news. What was the good news?

> *Then they found an Egyptian in a field and brought him to David; and they gave him bread and he ate, and they let him drink water. … Then David said to him: "To whom do you belong, and where are you from?" And he said, "I am a young man from Egypt, servant of an Amalekite; and*

my master left me behind, because three days ago I fell sick. We made an invasion of the southern area of the Cherethites, in the territory which belongs to Judah, and of the southern area of Caleb; and we burned Ziklag with fire." And David said to him, "Can you take me down to this troop?" So he said, "Swear to me by God that you will neither kill me nor deliver me into the hands of my master, and I will take you down to this troop." And when he had brought him down, there they were, spread out over all the land, eating and drinking and dancing, because of all the great spoil which they had taken from the land of the Philistines and from the land of Judah.

Then David attacked them from twilight until the evening of the next day. Not a man of them escaped, except four hundred young men who rode on camels and fled. So David recovered all that the Amalekites had carried away, and David rescued his two wives. And nothing of theirs was lacking, either small or great, sons or daughters, spoil or anything which they had taken from them; David recovered all. Then David took all the flocks and herds they had driven before those other livestock, and said, "This is David's spoil" (1 Samuel 30:11-20).

We are going to overtake the enemy and destroy him. His remnant will flee, and we will recover everything we lost. We are going to take great spoil. Don't interpret spoil as just earthly riches. Think about people, the people who are in bondage. The Word of God says, "*Where your treasure is, there is your heart also.*" (Mathew 19:21). God's heart is with His treasure, and treasure to God is people. We need to renew our minds and understand treasure in light of His heart, not our earthly lust. He said He would give us the nations for our inheritance.

Now David came to the two hundred men who had been so weary that they could not follow David, whom they also had made to stay at the Brook Besor. So they went out to meet David and to meet the people who were with him. And when David came near the people, he greeted them. Then all the wicked and worthless men of those who went with David answered and said, "Because they did not go with us, we will not give them any of the spoil that we have recovered, except for every man's wife and children, that they may lead them away and depart." (1 Samuel 30:21-22).

We see the same principle in the New Testament in the Book of Acts. The disciples and the apostles had everything in common. They shared with everyone as need required. What we find here in First Samuel is the establishment of this principle. Remember, David was a man after God's own heart. This being the case, we need to examine his life and discover what made him unique in his generation and model that in our own lives. Only the wicked and worthless men would not share their spoils.

But David said, "My brethren, you shall not do so with what the Lord has given us, who has preserved us and delivered into our hand the troop that came against us. For who will heed you in this matter? But as his part is who goes down to the battle, so shall his part be who stays by the supplies; they shall share alike" (1 Samuel 30:23-24).

There are those who engage in the battle, and those who stay behind and intercede. Both should be partakers of spoils and of everything that was stolen. They are to *all* share in everything alike. It doesn't matter if they are one day old in the Lord, their portion is going to be just as much as anyone else. That is God's

110

economy. We are about to take back everything the devil has stolen, along with the spoil. If the enemy has stolen loved ones, they are about to come back.

There was a woman who had debt of over $200,000, and her personal income was less than $35,000 a year. She faced foreclosure and a repossession of her assets. She was unable to declare bankruptcy because a portion of the debt was a federal student loan. The devil had stolen her peace, her rest, her joy, and her hope had been deferred making her heart sick. (see Prov. 13:12). She didn't know what to do.

At a service in her Church, the Lord gave me a word for her. I knew nothing of her financial situation. The Lord's word was this, "God is about to take care of a financial problem for you and you are going to be delivered." Two days later the federal government called her and erased the entire debt. She began to reap the spoils, and she took back what the enemy had stolen from her— joy, peace, and rest.

It is the Third Day. We are going to reap the spoils and take back everything the enemy has stolen from us and from our loved ones.

CHAPTER NINE

DEEPER THINGS

Restoration of the Vision in Wisdom

Now two women who were harlots came to the king and stood before him. And one woman said, "O my lord, this woman and I dwell in the same house; and I gave birth while she was in the house. Then it happened, the third day after I had given birth, that this woman also gave birth. And we were together; no one was with us in the house, except the two of us in the house. And this woman's son died in the night because she lay on him. So she arose in the middle of the night and took my son from my side, while your maidservant slept, and laid him in her bosom, and laid her dead child in my bosom. And when I rose in the morning to nurse my son, there he was, dead. But when I examined him in the morning, indeed, he was not my son whom I had borne. Then the other woman said, 'No! But the living one is my son, and the dead one is your son.' And the first woman said, 'No! But the dead one is your son, and the living one is my son.'" Thus they spoke before the king (1 Kings 3:16-22).

GOD HAS GRAFTED US, the Gentile Church, into the vine— into the Covenant People of God. Both groups of people are part of the same house. We have both given birth, but what will we do with our new life? We are to press into the promises of God. In this Scripture passage, a true provocation took place.

> *The king said, "The one says, 'This is my son, who lives, and your son is the dead one'; and the other says, 'No! But your son is the dead one, and my son is the living one.'" Then the king said, "Bring me a sword." (1 Kings 3:23-24).*

Now we know the sword of the Word rightly divides, piercing even to the division of soul and spirit, and of joints and marrow, and is a discerner of the thoughts and intents of the heart. (see Hebrews 4:12). There is a fuller release of this spiritual truth coming in this hour. The sword of the Spirit will rightly divide with greater clarity than we have known before with a corresponding release of supernatural wisdom.

> *...So they brought a sword before the king. And the king said, "Divide the living child in two, and give half to one and half to the other." Then the woman whose son was living spoke to the king, for she yearned with compassion for her son; and she said, "O my lord, give her the living child and by no means kill him!" But the other said, "Let him be neither mine nor yours, but divide him." So the king answered and said, "Give the first woman the living child and by no means kill him; she is his mother." And all Israel heard of the judgment which the king had rendered; and they feared the king for they saw that the wisdom of God was in him to administer justice (1 Kings 3:24-28).*

Both of these women spoke with passion. One spoke from envy and had impure motives, the other from a pure heart of love for her child. The wicked woman in this story is not so different

114

than many of us regarding our attitudes; "If I can't have it, you can't have it. If my ministry is going to die, so is yours."

And so the king stepped in. He rightly divided. He understood that both spoke with passion, but only one spoke with compassion. And rather than see the death of her son, the true mother of the child willingly released her infant—that ministry, that vision, that hope. With great wisdom the king discerned who the real mother of the child was. The test was not about whether he would divide the child. The test was to determine what was in the two women's hearts. What is in your heart?

RESTORATION OF WISDOM

In this Third Day, the wisdom of the King of kings is being released to us, His kings and priests. Isaiah writes about a supernatural wisdom written—the sevenfold spirit of God. We will be partakers of it and see it functioning in the Body of Christ fully as we progress towards the fulfillment of our destiny in this hour (see Isaiah 11:1-3). Supernatural wisdom is released to His people as we call upon Him for wisdom to rightly divide according to the Word of God and to discern the thoughts and intents of the heart.

We are in great need of wisdom in this hour because of what has been released on the earth. Jesus Himself said we are to be wise as serpents but harmless as doves (see Matt. 10:16). The devil is very crafty and his strategies are meticulously thought out and planned; plus he has had generations and thousands of years to practice. Without the supernatural release of God's wisdom into His church, we would be in dire straights against the wiles of such an enemy.

Throughout these Third Day promises God has been talking about supernatural release of strategies for overcoming in this hour. God has released tremendous wisdom as part of these strategies. Also on the Third Day, The fear of God will come upon all people. we will see the fear of God released in the churches as well as in the world. Jesus often demonstrated this wisdom when the Pharisees, Sadducees, and lawyers would test Him with questions. (Mark 12:13-17). They were unable to trap Him because of His answers, and they marveled at Him.

We need that kind of wisdom. When you and I begin to walk into the deeper things of God, the Pharisees and the Sadducees will confront us. They will nay-say and resist everything God has released to us. We must remember that they are not our enemy. Notice in the Scripture passage that Solomon did not administer judgment and penalty to the woman who lied—he didn't have to. Her sin was exposed. Nobody would trust her again. Supernatural wisdom is being released! It took that type of wisdom to discern between passion and compassion. And it became evident.

DEATH OF THE VISION

First Kings 3 speaks of the birth of the vision and the promised child born in the house. Then we saw the death of the vision and the promise. Next, we saw the theft of a vision and the promise. But this theft could not stand in the light of God's wisdom. Some of us have waited for the moment of birth, we have walked with the Lord and waited for God's timing. Some of us have given birth to a vision, and according to Genesis, we have to place that vision upon the altar where we will find out if we truly love the God of the promise more than the promise of God.

That's the death of the vision. Wisdom is necessary because many people will try and attach themselves to the anointing in your life, and steal that vision and promise. We need the wisdom of God to discern when this is the case. We have to be wise as serpents and harmless as doves. (Matt. 10:16). We have to know those who labor among us—this is extremely important. Even if someone we know and respect recommends a person to us, we still must get to know the person. Discernment is a priority in this hour.

Romans 8:26-27 says: *"Likewise the Spirit also helps in our weaknesses. For we do not know what we should pray for as we ought, but the Spirit Himself makes intercession for us with groanings which cannot be uttered. Now He who searches the hearts knows what the mind of the Spirit is, because He makes intercession for the saints according to the will of God."*

We must birth the vision of God in the closet of intercession. We have no concept of the extent of our calling and purpose. We must move past the place of involvement with menial, worthless things and spend time in the presence of God. It is in that intimate place that we receive direction, a strategy from God to birth and release the vision through groanings which cannot be uttered. Then comes the death of a vision.

Most assuredly, I say to you, unless a grain of wheat falls into the ground and dies, it remains along; but if it dies, it produces much grain. He who loves his life will lose it, and he who hates his life in this world will keep it for eternal life (John 12:24-25).

No matter what your calling, all of us go through the same process. We birth the vision through intercession and wrestling with God. Then the vision dies. It's the pattern of life. But from death comes a far greater harvest and far greater fruit than we could ever have accomplished without this process being fulfilled.

When we begin to walk out the birth of a vision, we walk in our own strength. We tend to reason things out. We do everything we know how to do, and that's okay. But there comes a time when God says, "You know what? I didn't call you to do this. You've got to let Me do this through you." The days of accomplishing the purpose of God with the arm of the flesh are over. His purpose for us is far beyond anything we could ever do. The Lord told me years ago: "I'm never going to ask you to do something you can do on your own, because if it's something you can do, it's not going to take any faith, and it's not going to be Me."

When everything He asks us to do is beyond our ability or our capability—at that juncture we must be on our face, constantly seeking God for wisdom and empowerment to accomplish what He's asking of us. If it's something you can do on your own, you better recheck the voice you hear. God always stretches us beyond what we are able to accomplish.

Foolish one, what you sow is not made alive unless it dies (1 Corinthians 15:36).

Recently, we have begun to experience amazing creative miracles. But it was not always so. I used to pray for many people and watch them get worse! I had no faith for the healing, and was highly intimidated by others in my life who had mentored me and walked in great anointing for healing and miracles. I would stay on the other side of the room and send people to them for prayers.

But God began to change something in my heart. I began to die to the fear of 'no results'. I died to the lack of faith and intimidation of others. I said, "God, if anything's going to happen here, it's got to be You and not me." The Spirit of God whispered to me, "It's about time!" I learned that day that I'm not responsible for the outcome. I'm responsible for obedience. And I will be persistent. Some of the great miracles we have seen have not been because we prayed and sent people on their way. If nothing happens, we pray again. Sometimes victory manifests itself only through persistence. It is not by works, not by might, not by power, but by the Spirit of God.

> *I am the good shepherd. The good shepherd gives His life for the sheep. But a hireling, he who is not the shepherd, one who does not own the sheep, sees the wolf coming and leaves the sheep and flees; and the wolf catches the sheep and scatters them. The hireling flees because he is a hireling and does not care about the sheep* (John 10:11-13).

The death of a vision requires your death, too. You must lay down your life in exchange for the life and destiny that God has called you to. You can't treat your calling as temporary. You can't walk in a vision of convenience, and plan to walk away if it dries up. Where God plants you, you have to say, "You know what, God? I'm going to stay here until the day I die unless You release me. I'm in for the long haul." Too many people are in for the short term, thinking that someday they will get a better offer. God is not schizophrenic. God will not call you to one place this week and another the next. That's not God—that's absolute immaturity. That attitude is symptomatic of being led by the flesh and not by the Spirit.

THEFT OF THE VISION

Then there's the theft of a vision. Jesus says in John 10-10: "*The thief does not come except to steal, and to kill, and to destroy. I have come that they may have life, and that they may have it more abundantly."*

There is a difference between the devil stealing and destroying, and your vision dying and coming forth in newness of life with a tremendous harvest and release. Jesus said *"I have come that you might have life and have it more abundantly."* The principle that speaks to this is: only through death will true life spring forth. Jesus died on the Cross for you and me to walk in newness of life, true life. Before we knew Jesus, we were in spiritual darkness or death, but life came from His death.

In ministry, the life of the ministry comes through the death of the person called to that place as they surrender to God. Anything other than that the enemy will try to steal, kill, or destroy. But he can't steal, kill, or destroy something that is dead. There is nothing there for him to hold onto—it's like Teflon. If it's ours, the enemy will want to play tug of war with us. We all feel the conflict and the tugs every day. Flesh gets involved, and we have to repent. We need to say, "God, it's not my problem, because it's not about me and it's not about my ministry. It is all about You."

WISDOM GOD'S WAY

You, therefore, who teach another, do you not teach yourself? You who preach that a man should not steal, do you steal? (Romans 2:21).

The Lord taught me this principle some years ago. He said, "First, I've got to form it in you before I can release it through you." If the reality and the revelation are not birthed in your Spirit, then all you are giving the people are empty words, and there is no seed in it, there's no life. But when God has birthed it in you, and it is released in you, then when you release it, life comes forth. First it has to be formed in you, and then it can be released through you to bring life.

> ...to another the working of miracles, to another prophecy, to another discerning of spirits, to another different kinds of tongues, to another the interpretation of tongues (1 Corinthians 12:10).

> For though by this time you ought to be teachers, you need someone to teach you again the first principles of the oracles of God; and you have come to need milk and not solid food. For everyone who partakes only of milk is unskilled in the word of righteousness, for he is a babe. But solid food belongs to those who are of full age, that is, those who by reason of use have their senses exercised to discern both good and evil (Hebrews 5:12-14).

You have come to need milk. They had something beyond milk, but they came back to needing milk. God have mercy on us for going backward instead of forward. What senses is this scripture talking about? Our five natural senses? No. It means that by experience or practice, we can learn to discern that which is true and that which is false. There is a gift of discerning the spirits, and the Spirit of God can impart this gift so you can spot that which is not of God 100 yards away. However, if we walk with God consistently, and spend time in His Word consistently, then we will begin to exercise our spiritual senses so we can know without question what is true and what is false.

There was a time in my life, because of wounding, when rejection covered me and blinded me to many things. How did that play out in my life? I needed to be someone's savior, their hero, if you will. This reasoning was a set-up for disaster. Once God pulled the scales off my eyes and showed me the scheme that was prevalent in my life, I was delivered of it through repentance, and confession. All generational curses were broken. The end result is that now I can clearly spot those types of situations and avoid them.

Before, I was blind. Why? My senses were exercised through experience. It was the hard way, but they were exercised. And now I can see and understand how it functions. I don't mean with the physical eyes, I mean with the eyes of the Spirit. This process of having our senses exercised can be a painful exercise but it is part of the process of setting us free.

> *When He had come to His own country, He taught them in their synagogue, so that they were astonished and said, "Where did this Man get this wisdom and these mighty works?"* (Matthew 13:54).

When was the last time that was said of you? Jesus said that greater things than He did we are going to do. On this Third Day, wisdom is being released in an unprecedented way. God is looking for a forerunner people who are going to walk in this type of wisdom. There will come a time when people will look at you and say, "We know who you are, where did you get that wisdom?" And they will be astonished!

They were astonished at King Solomon's wisdom when he asked for the sword to divide the baby between the two women claiming to be the mother. It was the first act he performed as king other than the dedication of the temple. It was his first act of justice. He sat on his throne in his kingly position where he discerned,

justly, with wisdom from God, and it brought a tremendous fear of God, not only to those who were present, but to those who heard what had taken place. It is a Third Day promise that we will do greater things than Christ, and one of the areas in which the church will begin to excel in this hour is in the application of God's wisdom in a very profound display. The world will take notice and it will cause many to wonder.

> *Therefore settle it in your hearts not to meditate beforehand on what you will answer; for I will give you a mouth and wisdom which all your adversaries will not be able to contradict or resist* (Luke 21:14-15).

The Lord opened my heart to this Scripture when I was 17 years of age. I knew that my spirit man needed the Word of God. Sometimes I would read the Word for hours, and it seemed as though my mind was totally unfruitful. But I trusted that I was benefiting from my reading and then I would notice that certain Scriptures jumped out. I could grab them because God spoke to me through them. I've learned that it was the Lord who gave me this insight and wisdom at an early age. Because of this understanding my life has benefited greatly over the years as I've trusted in His word, and the work it was doing in me, whether I "felt" like it or not. Now, I know to trust the Lord to fill my mouth with His wisdom when it is needed, and He has never failed me.

I used to be extremely shy—there wasn't enough money to pay me to stand up in front of people and speak. But because I knew my calling, I would allow myself to be placed in situations where I had no choice. With extreme fear and trembling I would speak before an audience. It wasn't the fear of God—it was fear of man. It came from my wounded spirit of rejection. To overcome,

I had to rely upon the Scripture. I would say, "God, I don't know how to put notes together. God, I don't know how to do this."

He said, "Don't worry, I'll handle it."

I gained the confidence in God's supernatural ability because it began to supersede my lack of ability. He gave me ability that wasn't mine. He still does. I came to trust totally on God, and He chose to speak through me. I thank God He is faithful to His Word.

The wisdom God gives is not man's wisdom. It's not intellectual knowledge gained from collegiate study. It is God's wisdom. God takes the foolish things of this world to confound the wise. When I get to the place when I understand that my wisdom is insignificant compared to the unlimited, unmatched wisdom of God, I say, "God, I need Your wisdom." James 1:5 says if any lacks wisdom let him ask of God who gives liberally. We are all in desperate need of a liberal dose of God's wisdom every day. No one can stand against the wisdom of God.

> *Now in those days, when the number of the disciples was multiplying, there arose a complaint against the Hebrews by the Hellenists, because their widows were neglected in the daily distribution. Then the twelve summoned the multitude of the disciples and said, "It is not desirable that we should leave the Word of God and serve tables"* (Acts 6:1-2).

Pastors, take this as encouragement. Your calling as pastors or ministers of God is to spend time in prayer and the Word. I love the story of a well-known pastor who gave himself to God from 8:30 in the morning until 12:30 every day. He said, "Nobody knock on the office, no phone calls, nothing. Just God and I."

From 12:30 until whenever—four or five—he would do other church business.

God began to give him tremendous revelation, and he stuck with the plan that God had given him. His church grew so large, and he became so busy that he neglected his morning time with the Lord. After about two or three years, the Holy Spirit convicted him, and he repented. He planned to stand up in front of the congregation and tell them what God said and if they left, well, that would be okay. So he told his church, "God had told me to devote my morning to Him and I've gotten away from that schedule in the last couple of years. I've got to repent before God and to you because I've given you second best. But starting today, I will not come into the office until 12:30. I will not have any interruptions." To his amazement the congregation stood up and cheered. We can too easily allow ourselves to become so busy about the little things that we don't have time to spend with God or to hear from Him. That is changing today, on this Third Day.

Therefore, brethren, seek out from among you seven men of good reputation, full of the Holy Spirit and wisdom, whom we may appoint over this business; but we will give ourselves continually to prayer and to the ministry of the Word (Acts 6:3-4).

Entry-level qualifications for ministry in the early church, just to wait on tables, was to be full of the Holy Spirit, of good reputation, and full of wisdom. We have seriously lowered the standard! Today we seek volunteers rather than those who are called. Volunteers in the day of adversity will go A.W.O.L. Those who are called will stay the course. That is the difference between a hireling and a true shepherd.

Unfortunately, we have lowered the standard in the church for those called even to the ministry of helps. And we need to repent because God is looking for men and women who He can appoint to a position of authority and responsibility. There are places for people to come alongside to help, but we've lowered the standard across the board. That doesn't fit Scriptural pattern. We need the fear of the Lord to come upon the church once again.

The fear of the Lord is the beginning of wisdom; and the knowledge of the Holy One is understanding (Proverbs 9:10).

We must have the fear of God in the church, and realize that what we say is heard by Heaven—and there are consequences. Example: There was a minister who believed that the gifts had passed away. A woman came into his church with cancerous tumors and asked for prayer. He prayed, and she was instantly healed! In the parking lot after church he ran into some of the elders who were very excited about the healing. Instead of rejoicing with them, he proclaimed that the incident was of the devil and not God. Within two hours he died. He blasphemed the Holy Spirit. He spoke against God, and there were consequences. It brought tremendous fear of God into that church. The fear of God is the beginning of wisdom. We need it.

Do not let your heart envy sinners but be zealous for the fear of the Lord all the day (Proverbs 23:17).

Be zealous for the fear of the Lord. Passionately pursue that place in God where you walk in the fear of the Lord. In all our passion and understanding, in all our petitions for "things," we need to get the fear of the Lord into our hearts. We need to walk in a place of respect and reverence for the Living God and His

Word. Not religious practice or simple recognition, but the practice of relationship with Him and recognition of Who He is.

We've had religious constraints placed upon us that became legalistic bondage rather than relational constraints that come from a heart of love and gratitude toward the Living God. There's a vast difference between the two. So the question is: where are you in this process? The birth of a vision, the death of a vision, or the theft of a vision? Hopefully, you are not the one stealing a vision. Let me say that you don't need to worry if someone tries to steal your vision. God will rightly judge each situation as it is presented to Him. Understand this: it must first be presented to Him just as the two women came before King Solomon for his judgment. Trust the King. Trust Him. But also trust the leaders He has put into your life because there is coming a release of supernatural wisdom and discernment.

> *In those days Hezekiah was sick and near death. And Isaiah the prophet, the son of Amoz, went to him and said to him, "Thus says the Lord: 'Set your house in order, for you shall die and not live.' Then he turned his face toward the wall and prayed to the Lord saying, 'Remember now, O Lord, I pray, how I have walked before You in truth and with a loyal heart, and have done what was good in Your sight.'" And Hezekiah wept bitterly. And it happened, before Isaiah had gone out into the middle court, that the Word of the Lord came to him, saying, "Return and tell Hezekiah the leader of My people, 'Thus says the Lord, the God of David your father: I have heard your prayer, I have seen you tears, surely I will heal you. On the third day you shall go up to the house of the Lord.'" (2 Kings 20:1-5).*

Sometimes intercession is a place of brokenness before God. Many leaders today are in a very precarious position. They have done everything they know to do, God's hand of blessing has been there, and yet God says, "You are going to die and not live." On this Third Day, there is a test coming to the hearts and the lives of leaders in the Kingdom. Hezekiah went to God and he lay before God in prayer, in the groanings of his innermost being, and cried out, "Lord, I've done everything I've know to do. I don't know how or why I might have failed you. But, God I've done everything I know how to do. I've tried to adhere to Your Word, I've tried to honor Your Word, I've tried to honor You in everything I've done. Lord God, what more can I do?"

There was a brokenness that entered his heart, one that needed to be present for the release of what God wanted to do in Hezekiah's life. Hezekiah could have become angry. God said he wept bitterly, but He did not say that he became bitter. He didn't have time. Immediately, Isaiah told him "God heard your intercessions. You are going to live and not die. He has given you fifteen more years."

Many in leadership now are in a place of transition. God desires to change their circumstance...change the wineskin... change their hearts. God doesn't always make His desires known through nice little notes saying, "I've got something new for you." He tests hearts—and sometimes that test comes through adversity. What is our response to adversity? What is our response to the furnace of affliction?

If we allow God to change our hearts even if in adversity, what is our benefit? The benefits are in the promise of the Third and seventh days...the promise of doing the same works of God and even greater ones!

> *Most assuredly, I say to you, he who believes in Me, the works that I do he will do also; and greater works than these he will do because I go to My Father. And whatever you ask in My name, that I will do, that the Father may be glorified in the Son* (John 14:12-13).

The Holy Spirit challenged me with a question—who did the miracles in the Old Testament? God the Father, God the Son, and God the Holy Spirit. Jesus! The works that He did we are going to do. He is the same yesterday, today, and forever! He is the same God in the Old Testament and the New Testament. The New covenant began with Jesus at Calvary. The Gospels are under the old covenant until His resurrection. Now we're in the new covenant.

Did you know that we can climb Mount Sinai and stand in the glory of the Living God? We can part the waters. We can walk so closely with God that we can be like Enoch and have Him take us home. (See Genesis 5:24.) It's our choice. Will we take it? Jude 1:14 says Enoch was the seventh from Adam (the seventh day). We are an end-time Enoch generation! He was a type and foreshadow of the seventh-day Christian. The question is, will we dare to believe that we can walk with God just as Enoch walked with God? Dare we believe that we have a unique and incredible destiny as a Third Day generation? I say yes! We dare to believe!

CHAPTER TEN

THE COMPLETED TEMPLE

Jesus in Residence

Then Tattenai, governor of the region beyond the River, Shethan-Boznai, and their companions diligently did according to what King Darius had sent. So the elders of the Jews built, and they prospered through the prophesying of Haggai the prophet and Zechariah the son of Iddo. And they built and finished it, according to the commandment of the God of Israel, and according to the command of Cyrus, Darius, and Artaxerxes king of Persia. Now the temple was finished on the third day of the month of Adar, which was in the sixth year of the reign of King Darius. Then the children of Israel, the priests and the Levites and the rest of the descendants of the captivity celebrated the dedication of this house of God with joy (Ezra 6:13-16).

LET ME FIRST ESTABLISH WHO THE TEMPLE IS. First Corinthians 6:19 tells us: "*Or do you not know that your body is the temple of the Holy Spirit who is in you, whom you have from God, and you are not your own?*"

We are the temple of God! The prophetic picture is clear. The temple historically was completed on the Third Day. The temple of the Holy Spirit that we are will also be completed on *this* Third Day. This is not only speaking of the Church corporately, but also each of us as an individual expression of God's corporate temple as well. This is an incredible promise! It will take a miraculous transformation by the Spirit of God to cause what we now perceive as the Church to become an entity that is without spot and without wrinkle. This will be a Body of believers that will exemplify Christ-like character. A mature son of God! God will finish what He began because on the Third Day, the temple will be completed.

We know that the Church will be caught away to meet the Lord in the air. Whether we believe in the pre, mid, or post tribulation rapture should not be our main concern. Our focus must be upon the mandate given to the Church by the Lord: *"Be ye holy even as I Am Holy."* (1 Peter 11:16) One thing is certain, today is all we have, and today we must work out our own salvation with fear and trembling (Phil. 2:12). Today we must pursue the Lord with all of our hearts.

Today I must make a choice—all of Him and none of me, or, all of me and little to none of Him. Today, I must press toward the mark of the high calling of God in Christ Jesus. Today, as I hear His voice, I must not harden my heart. Today is all I have! Tomorrow is not sure, and yesterday is past, therefore I must live this day to its fullest looking for the coming of the Lord *today*. If I do this, He *will* find faith in the earth when He comes back!

When I worked at TBN in the late 1970s, we would often have several different prophecy teachers as guests. There were pre-trib, post-trib, mid-trib teachers all with very compelling arguments and insights into the Scripture as to why they were correct in their assessment of when and how, during the tribulation period, Jesus would be returning.

As a young Christian, I was very confused! They all seemed to be right, and yet they didn't agree! As I turned to the Lord for clarification, He said to me, "It's very simple. I'm coming today! Today is all you have and I said to you that you must always be looking for my coming. Live this day as if I were returning today and you will always be prepared."

If Jesus came today, right this minute, would you be ready? We must live our lives as if He is coming right now! If we do that, it will change our lives. We won't be as concerned with much of what currently has our focus and attention. We will have joy and peace while living in anticipation and expectation. We will see with greater clarity the prophetic signs of the times and be fully engaged in the work of the Lord. Our heart and focus will be on the Kingdom that is above, and there we will store our treasure. (See Matthew 6:34.)

> *So they rose early in the morning and went out into the Wilderness of Tekoa; and as they went out, Jehoshaphat stood and said, "Hear me, O Judah and you inhabitants of Jerusalem: Believe in the Lord your God, and you shall be established; believe His prophets, and you shall prosper"* (2 Chronicles 20:20).

> *So the elders of the Jews built, and they prospered through the prophesying of Haggai the prophet and Zechariah the son of Iddo...* (Ezra 6:14).

As we learn to discern the times and seasons as did Ezra and the children of Israel, we must also learn to discern the voice of God when He speaks through His prophets. It is in heeding these prophetic mandates that we will prosper in what we do. We must learn to discern, however, because not everybody who labels himself (or herself) as a prophet is a prophet.

Character and fruit defines gift. Gift does not define character and fruit. Many have seen those with tremendous gifts flowing in their lives and yet there was no evidence of the fruit of righteousness nor was there evidence of the character of Christ. At the same time, I've seen character and fruit evidenced in the lives of some saints as they are content to live in obscurity, giving the Lord all the glory for any accomplishments in and through their lives. There are many, many false prophets and lying signs and wonders right now...and more will be released.

Let me share with you one of the indicators that causes me to beware: when I see someone in ministry who has to tell you how anointed they are or how profoundly they flow in the prophetic, or anyone who has to "toot their own horn," I take a step back and discern what is going on. I also look for fruit that remains from their ministry. Perhaps this person is just immature. Or there is a need in their life that should be recognized. It might even be that the person is caught up in our Western success mindset and thinks that the more notoriety received, the greater the ministry.

There can be any number of scenarios that makes a person do what they do. The bottom line: we must learn to walk in a spirit of discernment. We *must* increase in the area of discernment. We must seek for and cultivate the wisdom that only God can give.

Only then will we be in a position to judge the fruit accurately and impartially. This will keep us in the place of fruitfulness and will position us to prosper in all that the Lord has for us.

His parents went to Jerusalem every year at the Feast of the Passover. When Jesus was twelve years old, they went up to Jerusalem according to the custom of the feast. When they had finished the days, as they returned, the Boy Jesus lingered behind in Jerusalem. And Joseph and His mother did not know it; but supposing Him to have been in the company, they went a day's journey, and sought Him among their relatives and acquaintances (Luke 2:41-44).

Pay close attention to this lesson: many churches suppose that Jesus is with them. They say to themselves, "God is blessing us, we're doing what is right." They are unaware that He is not present among them. Let that reality sink into your heart.

*So when they did not find Him, they returned to Jerusalem, seeking Him. Now so it was that after **three days** they found Him in the temple (Luke 2:45)*

On the Third Day the temple will be complete, and Jesus will be found in the temple. I used to pray, "Lord, I just want more of You." That's not in my vocabulary anymore. It's all or nothing. It's got to be *all* of you, God, and *none* of me. The church in this last hour will be all of Him and none of this flesh. When men and women look at you they will not see you, they will see Jesus in you. They won't remember your name and your face, but they will remember that Jesus visited them and the Kingdom of God has come near. God's "secret service" is not only alive and well, but it is increasing as Christians begin to realize "it's all about Him!" We've built names and ministries and dynasties…we've merchandised the anointing. But the heart of the Father is all of Him and none of us.

Paul understood that principle. At the beginning of his ministry, though, it was, "Some of You and some of me." As he journeyed on in the Lord, he said, "Lord more of you and less of me." By the end of his life he said, "Lord all of You and none of me." This is a snapshot of spiritual maturity. On this Third Day, the temple corporately and you as the temple of God individually, will be completed, and Jesus will be found in His temple. We are positioned right now for a major change and transformation in the Body of Christ.

THE WISDOM OF JESUS

Jesus displayed tremendous wisdom—He confounded the teachers.

> …*they found Him sitting in the midst of the teachers, both listening to them and asking them questions. And all who heard Him were astonished at His understanding and answers. So when they saw Him, they were amazed; and His mother said to Him, "Son, why have You done this to us? Look, Your father and I have sought You anxiously"* (Luke 2:46-48).

The second-day church has been asking, "Lord, why are you doing things that way? You're supposed to be with us, journeying with us. We know the way—we've been this way many times before."

> *And He said to them, "Why did you seek Me? Did you not know that I must be about My Father's business?"* (Luke 2:49).

There is a diametric change coming. There is Kingdom business, and there is church business. Kingdom business is different than church business. Sometimes church business lines itself up with Kingdom business, but the change coming will bring a huge realignment of the way we function. When revival comes, it can be messy, and it is sometimes unpleasant. God will offend our senses to reveal our heart. What is decent and in order to the Lord is not necessarily what we would consider decent and in order. God places leadership to steward what He does and to discern, but not to interfere. Remember that the wheat and the tares always grow together. And the tares will not want what God is planning to do.

"Well, what about all that flesh? What if the revival gets out of hand and everyone starts acting weird?"

People always have an opinion. Opinions aren't productive. There was a lot of controversy over the 1994 revival in Toronto, Canada. I heard that it was the devil, and I heard excited reports about God moving. People would continually ask my opinion regarding what was happening there. Well, I wasn't there, so I had no basis upon which to form an opinion. Had I tried, it would have been conjecture on my part, and I would have been speaking about something I knew nothing about.

When there are many manifestations that have both flesh and Holy Spirit, we need to keep silent. We have to "hold fast what is good" and reject the rest. We cannot allow ourselves to enter into gossip or conjecture. We must learn to walk in wisdom and understand that we do not always have to have an opinion. The wheat and tares grow together. We should not make something our concern or problem that rightfully we have no business speaking into in the first place. Judgment belongs to the Lord.

Brother Seymour, in the Azuza Street revival, understood the principle of the wheat and tares growing together. God cautioned him and warned him not to address error—He would take care of it. Brother Seymour was to steward the revival and what God was doing. However, because of outside pressure, after a few years Brother Seymour began to address those things that were seemingly offensive, and it wasn't long before the revival ceased.

When the harvest comes in a revival, God sends His angels to cut away the tares. This is not to say that we should not discern what is of God and what isn't. I'm not saying that we should not deal with demonic manifestations. What I am saying: if our focus moves from what the Lord is doing to addressing every little fleshly outburst, we will miss what the Lord is trying to do. We must keep our hearts focused on the Lord. Stand back and watch. God is perfectly capable of handling anything that crops up!

I was privileged to attend a "Catch the Fire" conference some years ago where the "Toronto Blessing" stream was flowing. During the worship, a person in front of me was operating with a familiar spirit, mocking the Lord. My spirit was grieved within me as I was trying to worship. Quietly under my breath, I took authority over the spirit, and I told the person to sit down and be still. Immediately, that person sat down and for the rest of the meeting never said another word. I know the person didn't hear me because the music was so loud I couldn't even hear myself. But I do know that the spirit that was operating in the person was subject to the authority of Christ and the blood of the Lamb. There was no need to make a public spectacle. We do not wrestle against flesh and blood, but against principalities, powers, and the rulers of darkness of this world.

Another mistake many make is trying to bind an operation of the flesh. You cannot override an individual's will. If someone is operating in the flesh, we need to instruct them in love and teach them truth. Most of the time if an individual is operating in the flesh they either want attention, they want to fit in, or they are trying to connect with God in the only way they know how. And lastly, we do not want to make the mistake of trying to bind the Spirit of God in operation lest we grieve the Holy Spirit.

We must become people who learn to discern what is happening around us and to respond accordingly. I've tested this all over the world in countries that are full of witchcraft. From America to Third World nations, it works. We have authority. If leadership would exercise their authority before a service begins, there would be a lot less confusion during a service.

On the Third Day, Jesus will be found in the temple, reasoning with the teachers and with those who are seeking to know Him. He will impart revelation that will amaze and astonish us. When John and Peter were taken before the Sanhedrin (the Pharisees, Sadducees, and the lawyers) because of the miracles that they accomplished, the statement was made that they recognized that they were ignorant and unlearned men...but they had been with Jesus. (See Acts chapter 3.)

What set them apart from the norm was the time they spent with Jesus. The Pharisees, the religious leaders, recognized Jesus in them because they knew they could not have obtained that wisdom from normal schooling. The Lord is about to release that manifestation of Himself in us—the release of wisdom that defies the norm, a wisdom that cannot come from books or degrees or great universities. We've got to give Him the key that allows Him free access to all of our heart. We must give Him permission to be "God" in us and let Him be "God" through us! We must come to the place of brokenness in our own lives and our own efforts and pray, "All of you Lord and none of me, I just want to be like Jesus."

I remember hearing a prophetic word about a person's journey in life. This person and Jesus were walking down the path of life and all of a sudden the picture transformed into just one person walking—Jesus. When the person turned around to look, he could still see the eyes of the person who had been walking alongside Jesus. He (Jesus)smiled and waved and walked farther down life's journey. Just before he got out of sight, he turned around once again and Jesus had completely replaced the person, no longer could you see the man's eyes looking out through Jesus. All you could see was Jesus. That should be our passion and our pursuit. All of Him, and none of us!

The Lord spoke to me one day and said, "I want you to lose your individuality but you can keep your personality." We are part of a Body. Can you imagine when God finally does what He said He's going to do? The Church will be one, flowing together— each person in their file and their rank without any conflict or any breaking of ranks. What is that going to look like? It will be incredible…supernatural.

> *Do you not know that you are the temple of God and the Spirit of God dwells in you? If anyone defiles the temple of God, God will destroy them. For the temple of God is holy, which temple you are* (1 Corinthians 3:16-17).

The Third Day and the seventh day coincide, but in the seventh day we are required to be holy just like we were on the Third Day. This "temple" (you and I) is going to be holy on the Third Day. That is the only way Jesus will be found there. Just as the second-day church has been sensing a strange "something is missing," feeling because they don't realize that Jesus is not there, so the Third Day church will be the church where Jesus is found reasoning with His people and opening His Word to them.

Some of you in this season are going to have "suddenlies" in your life, visitations from God that will transform your life. The Lord is redeeming the time. We are in a season of an incredible release of the wisdom of God, the fear of God, and godly discernment. This Third Day will see the sons and daughters of God coming to maturity. We will be a people who will be holy and pure before Him. This is the day that all of creation has been groaning for and awaiting: the coming forth of the mature sons and daughters of God!

As mentioned previously, if we allow God to change our hearts even if it's in adversity, the benefits are in the promise of the Third and seventh days—the promise of doing the same works of God and even greater ones!

> *"Most assuredly, I say to you, he who believes in Me, the works that I do he will do also; and greater works than these he will do because I go to My Father. And whatever you ask in My name, that I will do, that the Father may be glorified in the Son."* (John 14:12-13).

CHAPTER ELEVEN

THE ROYAL ROBES

Heirs of the Kingdom, Destiny of the Third Day Church

ROSH HASHANAH, September 7, 2002, radically and definitively changed my life. We pray and pray for intimacy with God, but we really have no clue what that means or what it may entail. I had always told the Lord that if He ever got close enough for me to grab hold of, I would never let Him go. But when the opportunity actually came, and God physically embraced me, I was completely undone. Suddenly I was filled and empty at the same time. I was full and hungry. I didn't know if it lasted for a moment or an eternity, as time completely stood still. He released gifts and prophetic insight that spoke to the day and hour in which we currently live. Gifts and insight so unfathomable, words can't express it. And this is what He is giving to the Body of Christ right now. It is more than a Divine Romance, it is complete unity with the King of kings on a level never before experienced. And it is powerful!

A lot of the Third Day Scriptures say *it came to pass on the Third Day*. So it's either going to come to pass, or it will happen on the third day.

*It happened **on the third day** that Esther put on her royal robes and stood in the inner court of the king's palace across from the king's house while the king sat on his royal throne in the royal house facing the entrance of the house* (Esther 5:1).

The process that Esther went through in preparation just to meet the king has great significance in our own process of sanctification. Each one of us as believers in Christ has been walking out a process. We've been on a journey of becoming more like Him. He is after Christ-like character in us. He is not impressed with our gifts or the lack of gifts. What is most important to Him is a passion to be like Jesus.

If Esther is the type of the Church or the Body of Christ, what does that royal robe signify? We know that robes and mantles in the Word of God speak of anointing and gifts. They speak of position and God's government. This was not a common mantle or a robe. Esther is clothed in *royal* clothing. There is a release of destiny in this hour. With that release of destiny is a release of the mantle of the King of glory Himself.

This experience I am going to explain has already happened. I was told that I was a forerunner and that this encounter I had with the Lord was significant of what the Lord was releasing in the church as a whole.

One of the very first things in my experience on Rosh Hashanah was that when the Lord came to me, and after He hugged me, I was frozen in place and could not move. The angels of God came up behind me and put a purple robe on my shoulders. I was, for lack of a better expression, extremely agitated. I thought, "Hey, guys, He's over there, you missed."

But God had a plan and a purpose for their actions. The royal robe speaks of a mantle that comes with maturity. Remember adoption according to the ancient belief system? You were born into the family of God. We all have been born into His family through the blood of Jesus. In the natural world, a father and mother had a child born unto them. When that child became of age and was mature enough to participate in the family business, mature enough to walk with the authority of the family, then that child was adopted by the same parents to become a joint heir. When we are mature in our walk with Christ, we move from being just children of the King, to mature joint heirs.

That is the same relationship portrayed in Esther. Out of all of the beautiful young virgins who came before the king, only one caught his attention. One was crowned with favor in the courts before she even met him, because the eunuch knew there was something special about her. There is something special about a man or a woman today that has a passionate desire for God. There is great favor being released upon them, and they are about to come into their inheritance—the place of maturity where the royal robe will be placed upon them.

Esther put on her royal robes and stood in the inner court of the king's palace. The inner court was directly across from the place where the king sat on his royal throne. Esther realized that her actions were contrary to court protocol and that she could just as easily provoke the king to disfavor and dishonor rather than being the recipient of his favor. There was something, however, that compelled her to action.

Not only did she have a God-given destiny, she also had a passion to see that destiny fulfilled as well as a compassion for her people. She understood that her position was a platform from which she could fulfill the mandate of Heaven and see her generation saved. The seriousness of the challenge caused her to fast and pray for three days, and on the third day she obtained the favor of the king! One of the keys to her receiving favor: *she was not trying to obtain favor for herself, but as a means to intercede and stand in the gap for her people.* Hers was a selfless act!

What would happen if coming before the Throne of Grace we had a 50 percent chance of favor or disfavor, life or death? Do you think we would become a little bit more passionate and focused in our Christian lives? Do you think perhaps we would learn what it is that moves the heart of the King and not be so quick to approach His throne with our petty, selfish desires?

In her place as the queen, Esther stood before the king on behalf of her people. She stood in the gap at great risk to her own life. The mantle, the robe, the royal apparel will not be given to just anybody. It will be given to those who have already found favor with God, and who are willing to lay down their lives on behalf of another. That eliminates a lot of latter day ministries who think ministry is all about them and not about God or others.

Esther counted the cost. She didn't count her life dear, and she stood and waited for the verdict. The weight of her people's situation caused her to come on behalf of a people who were about to perish at the decree of a madman. She was willing to die! The question we need to ask ourselves: *am I willing to lay down my life in order to fulfill my destiny by standing in the gap for a lost and dying generation?*

So it was when the king saw Queen Esther standing in the court that she found favor in his sight and the king held out to Esther the golden scepter that was in his hand. Then Esther went near and touched the top of the scepter (Esther 5:2).

Esther and Mordecai had a destiny and their destiny was not to live in the lap of luxury because she had now become queen. Their destiny involved pleading the Jews' cause before the king, even if it required the laying down of their own lives. Most people believe that receiving God's favor means getting as many worldly possessions as we can, but this is not the testimony of Scripture as Esther's life proves. She had a passion. She had a destiny. As this situation unfolded, she came to the realization, before the third day, that her destiny was to stand in the gap for her people.

That is our destiny as well. Our lives are to be laid down on behalf of a people whom God desires to save in this hour. And the greatest anointing, the greatest mantles, the greatest giftings will go to those who are willing to lay down their lives and count everything loss for the sake of the gospel and for winning the lost.

"…Whatever you wish Queen Esther. What is your request? It should be given to you up to half the kingdom!" So Esther answered, "If it pleases the king, let the king and Haman come today to the banquet that I have prepared for him." Then the king said, "Bring Haman quickly that he may do as Esther has said." So the king and Haman went to the banquet that Esther had prepared (Esther 5:3-5).

God says we're to be wise as serpents and harmless as doves. (Matt. 10:16). Esther knew that wisdom would be required to accomplish her purpose. She made the feast in honor of the king himself, and invited Haman to give him an opportunity to repent.

Haman is a type of the believer who has the wrong motive in his heart, a person who is puffed up with pride and arrogance.

Think about some of our attitudes; "I'm just as gifted as that person, why doesn't God use me?" or, "I do more in this church than anyone else and nobody notices my sacrifice." I could go on and on, but I think you get the picture.

These types of attitudes are rampant in the church today. But there is a hidden remnant who has labored long and hard in the wilderness never asking for any of the accolades of man or the rewards of this life. They have been performing their duty to God solely on the basis of their love for Him. These will be brought to the king's attention like Mordecai. The king took out the book of remembrances because he couldn't sleep one night and said,

"Whatever happened to Mordecai? You know he saved my life. And he didn't ask for anything, but what did we do for him?"

And the servant said, "Nothing."

And the king said "Oh, that's not right. Let's ask Haman what we should do for somebody like that." (Esther 6:1-6, Paraphrase mine.)

Haman arrogantly believed the king was talking about him. Pay attention to this type of spiritual arrogance and blindness. There is about to be a shifting of the wealth in the church. For those who have promoted the "gospel of mammon" and perpetrated a false gospel to gain influence and wealth, God is about to strip them bare, and release their wealth to those who, in humility, have been hidden away doing the work that God has called them to do. If the motive is wrong, God will expose it.

He has already raised up Esthers and Mordecais in secret places, and they will fulfill their destinies with righteousness, holiness, purity, and the fear of God. It's the Third Day and we are going to be dressed in the royal garments of the court of the King, and we will be willing to lay down our lives before the King on behalf of the people.

> *At the banquet of wine the king said to Esther "What is your petition? It should be granted to you. What is your request? Up to half the kingdom it shall be done." "If I have found favor in the sight of the king and if it pleases the king to grant my petition and fulfill my request then let the king and Haman come to the banquet which I will prepare for them and tomorrow I will do as the king has said. I will tell you what my petition is"* (Esther 5:6-8).

Twice the king extended great favor to Esther. Two is the number of witness. And the outcome of that favor? Haman was exposed, Mordecai was elevated, and God positioned Esther and Mordecai for promotion so that they could stand in the gap for a nation and see it delivered from all of its enemies.

A Changed Heart for a Divine Purpose and Destiny

Jeremiah 29:11 says: *"For I know the thoughts that I think toward you says the Lord. Thoughts of peace and not of evil to give you a future and a hope."*

The Lord says He knows the thoughts that He thinks toward you: thoughts of peace and not of evil, to give you a future and a hope. Our future and hope is in Him. The Word says, "Where your heart is, that's where your treasure is." One day I asked God what treasure was to Him. He spoke to me clearly and said, "People are my treasure."

I told the Lord that I wanted to be like my Father in Heaven, and I prayed that He would change my heart to treasure what He treasures—people. I wish I could say it was instant, but very few things in my life have been instant. Even failure wasn't instant. It has been a process of having my spiritual eyes opened and my heart exposed, so I can align myself with the Father's heart and become more like Him.

Because of my many experiences with the heavenly realm and the Lord Himself, the spiritual realm is becoming more real than the natural in many ways. You may have training manuals that teach you how to hear the voice of God better or understand the Word of God more fully, but our spiritual senses must be cultivated. We must choose to move out of our daily routine into that place where our hearts and attention are on God.

There are times we go about our everyday business, and we don't think about spiritual things. When we decide that today we are going to focus our attention and heart on God, then all of a sudden those spiritual senses kick in. It could be that you receive discernment or some other special sense needed at the exact moment. Live in expectancy of these manifestations, and push toward exercising those gifts and senses. You will grow hungry for more of those experiences, not for the sake of the experience alone, but because you will see lives change before your eyes.

We have a destiny to change lives, to bring the light of the glory of God to a dark world. As we press toward the goal—to be conformed to His image. The gifts and anointing, spiritual acuity, and all of our spiritual senses will become more sensitive to the realm of the Spirit. As we begin to exercise our spiritual gifts and operate with greater sensitivity, the Lord releases us to touch people at a deeper level and see them set free from afflictions and bondages. I've heard of instances where an individual's sensitivity has become so acute that they are overwhelmed and ask the Lord to "shut it off." We must count the cost before we enter into the race! We cannot set our hand to the plow and then turn back.

Yielding to the Lord requires a willingness to sacrifice our security in order to see others free. We become vessels of life, and no longer a stumbling block to life. Like Esther, you walk in the destiny you are called to rather than the self you are called out of.

Notice that the scepter the king extended was gold, which speaks of the purity of God's favor. One of the things that the angels placed on my head on Rosh Hashanah was a golden crown, the crown of favor. We are crowned with favor on the Third Day.

On the seventh day the heart of the king was merry... (Esther 1:10).

It was on the seventh day that the king took away Vashti's crown and gave it to Esther. There was a changing of the guard on the seventh day—we are in the seventh day and the Third Day. There is a change taking place. Why? Because Vashti refused the command of the king. The Church today is in the same position. Be warned, it can happen to us—*those who refuse the commands of the King will lose their crowns and the priviledge of ruling with Him.*

An aid to help us obey the Lord, so we can keep our crowns is found in Psalm 139:17-18, *"How precious also are your thoughts to me, O God! How great is the sum of them! If I should count them, they would be more in number than the sand. When I awake I am still with You."*

When I'm asleep, I'm still with Him. Try this as an experiment. *Ask God to speak to you in the night seasons.* He never sleeps, you know. He can and will train you. Often it is easier for the Lord to speak to us during our sleeping hours when all noise and outside distractions are removed. Not only is this a biblical way for the Lord to communicate with His people, it is an increasing means that the Lord is using in this hour to communicate His plans and purposes to His people.

Esther and Mordecai were raised up for a specific purpose on the Third Day. She received favor, and that favor brought about the destruction of the enemy of God's people. Today, all of us have enemies. And though we don't wrestle against flesh and blood, there are situations and things in your life that are enemies to the destiny God has for you. It might even be your flesh. God is lifting up a standard within us. He is raising up a standard to stand in the gap and take down the enemies that are destroying God's people.

> *On that day King Ahasuerus [Xerxes] gave Queen Esther the house of Haman, the enemy of the Jews…* (Esther 8:1)

Not only did Esther and Mordecai stand in the gap willing to lay down their lives, they won the victory and reaped the spoils. Mordecai became second in command to the king. Esther is a type of intercessor. Mordecai is a type of warrior. The intercessors always precede what God is doing, to open the path for the warriors to come in.

> *And Mordecai came before the king for Esther had told how he was related to her. So the king took off his signet ring which he had taken from Haman and gave it to Mordecai.*

And Esther appointed Mordecai over the house of Haman (Esther 8:2).

The signet ring means the absolute authority of the king. If any decree, anything he had written, was stamped with his signet ring it became law. God has released His authority to mature sons and daughters to a degree we've never experienced. And when we speak or decree the decree of God, it is done! The releasing of authority is done by God's decree, by His command only.

For example, I was ministering in Grand Forks, British Columbia, Canada—a small Canadian city located on what is known as a "lay line." That is a specific place used by witches (those who practice Wicca and shamanism) to operate in astral-projection, or "teleportation." One morning at 4 A.M. an intercessor named Eleanor Theisen went to her church to pray. As she left her home, a fog surrounded her, and a warlock appeared in the gloom. She sensed evil, but was not afraid. She applied the blood of Jesus, and the warlock immediately disappeared. That same afternoon, a Buddhist monk appeared out of nowhere, pacing in front of her home, chanting incantations. That evening, the Lord told me to perform a prophetic act: take a flaming sword approximately four feet long and sever the lay line. I obeyed.

The result was immediate and rippled through the community. All of a sudden the spiritual atmosphere changed, and the witches and warlocks could no longer wield the power they had been accustomed to. There was a great flurry of activity in and about that small community as they tried to once again dominate that region. My friend Pastor Ron Legary, and his congregation have continued to stand in victory in that region for a number of years now.

God is releasing a greater measure of authority on this Third Day, and we must understand that when we decree something it is finished! But only when God tells us to—remember: *speak when spoken through*. To walk in authority, you must be under authority. Nobody is an authority to themselves. There is tremendous liberty and freedom in God's authority having control over your life.

> *Now Esther spoke again to the king, fell down at his feet, and implored him with tears to counteract the evil of Haman the Agagite, and the scheme which he had devised against the Jews. And the king held out the golden scepter toward Esther...* (Esther 8:3-4).

Look closely at the outcome here. Not only did her intercessions destroy the enemy, she reversed the decrees that went forth.

> *So Esther arose and stood before the king and said, "If it pleases the king, and if I have found favor in your sight and that thing seems right to the king and I am pleasing in his eyes, let it be written to revoke the letters devised by Haman the son of Hammedatha, the Agagite, which he wrote to annihilate the Jews who were in all the king's provinces. For how can I endure to see the evil that will come to my people? Or how can I endure to see the destruction of my countrymen?" Then King Ahasuerus [Xerxes] said to Queen Esther and Mordecai the Jew, "Indeed I have given Esther the house of Haman, and they have hanged him on the gallows because he tried to lay his hand on the Jews. You yourself write a decree as you please. You yourself write a decree in the king's name and seal it with the king's signet ring; for a letter which is written in the king's name and sealed with the king's signet ring, no one can revoke"* (Esther 8:4-8).

Mature sons and daughters of God will walk with authority because of compassion and willingness to lay down their lives. They receive the favor of the King and the greatest anointing that can ever be released—the royal robes! Some would argue that we already have royal robes because we are saved; however, there is a requisite level of maturity that is required in order to walk in this type of authority. On this Third Day, we will become a people who will do the greater works that Jesus talked about in John 14:12. This promise has not been fulfilled in its entirety or to the degree it will be fulfilled in this generation. On the Third Day, the temple is going to be finished, and Jesus is going to be found in the temple. The former and latter rain is upon us; the royal robes have been given. God's favor is extended; and the signet ring of God's authority has now been placed upon our fingers. It is time for us to release the Kingdom of Heaven on earth and to walk as mature sons and daughters of God.

RAISED UP FOR THE LATTER AND FORMER RAINS

*Come, and let us return to the Lord. For He has torn but He will heal us; He has stricken but He will bind us up. After two days He will revive us; on the **third day** He will raise us up that we might live in his sight* (Hosea 6:1-2).

The word raise in this passage infers "coming to a place" of maturity where we can live in His sight or come constantly and consistently into the very throne room of God. It's about time we had a heavenly perspective of earth instead of an earthly perspective of Heaven! He will raise us up in this hour so we can live in His sight.

In the Book of Revelation, the seven churches were praised for their efforts, but every one of them fell short in some respect.

If Jesus is coming back for a Church without spot or wrinkle, whatever was wrong with the seven churches at that time will be dealt with on that day.

Our character must be changed to the extent that we can live in His sight. We are to be clothed in the glory of the Living God. So how do we transition from one place to the other? We can receive revelation, anointing, you name it, but the bottom line is: *He is the only One who can do anything.* We receive and participate in His Kingdom only because of His amazing grace, the unlimited, unmerited favor of God. God's supernatural ability overshadows your lack of ability so you can do what you could not do previously. It's a supernatural impartation to you so you can fulfill what you are called to do, and in some cases, it is without measure.

Pursue the knowledge of the Lord. His going forth is established as the morning, He shall come to us like the rain, like the latter and former rains of the earth, on this Third Day. The greatest awakening, the greatest move of God the world has ever seen is here—*now*. The final harvest! The conclusion of all things He began.

Joel 2:23 says: "*Be glad then you children of Zion, and rejoice in the Lord your God, for He has given you the former rain faithfully and He will cause the rain to come down for you—the former rain, and the latter rain in the first month.*"

We already know what day it is, the Third Day. Listen to the sound of the abundance of rain! This is not for the future, it is for now. It is the sovereign work and move of God. Recently, I have seen seven people healed who were diagnosed with fibromyalgia. Shortly we will see people with Down's syndrome healed.

Quadriplegics will walk out of their wheelchairs. This will not be a small trickle of rain; it will be a downpour. It will be an outpouring of incredible signs, wonders, and miracles unlike anything we've ever seen or heard of in scope and frequency. The "norm" will be those who are healed and set free while the rare case will be those who do not receive their healing. The "norm" will be untold salvations and visitations of the Lord.

The threshing floors shall be full of wheat and the vats shall overflow with new wine and oil (Joel 2:24).

The harvest is here. The fields are ripe. Pray that the Lord will find laborers for the harvest. My dad had a pastor friend in Florida who lived in Africa for several years. During one of his crusades, he was preaching on the love and power of Christ, and that, "*with God, all things are possible*" (Mark 10:27).

During the meeting a lady in a wheelchair made her way to the ministry area in front of the platform. While the minister was speaking, she challenged him, shouting, "You say your God has power to forgive sins and heal people. Have Him heal my legs!" She pulled the blanket off her partially covered wheelchair and to the amazement of everyone, she had no legs! They had been amputated. Dad's friend, Smitty, paused for a moment and cried out, "Father, in Jesus' name I command legs to come forth on this woman now!" While he was still speaking, the lady forcefully pushed herself up and out of the wheelchair. In midair, before thousands of people, two new legs complete with feet and toes, grew forth and thousands ran forward to give their hearts to Jesus. That is the sound of the abundance of rain!

Every Christian needs to walk in that abundance of rain. We've been beaten up and afflicted, but now we can be healed by the Living God! Once we are healed, we need to take Him to the streets. Freely we have received, now we have to freely give. And we can go with the full assurance and understanding that the former and the latter rain are being poured out in this hour. We are clothed in royal robes, and we have been granted favor by God to accomplish our God-given destiny. We have come to the Kingdom for such a time as this! (Esther 4:14). The nations, the people of the world are our inheritance. They are the treasure of the Lord of Heaven. This is where ours hearts need to be focused—upon His treasure, so that the abundance of rain is seen on the earth in this Third Day.

I will restore to you... (Joel 2:25).

God is about to restore to you on this Third Day the years you thought were wasted. The years of struggle. The years of poverty. The years of trials and testings. God is about to restore to you the years it has taken you to get to the place where you are today. It will be done suddenly. One minute things look the same, the next minute things are restored. It is a Third Day promise you can count on.

You shall eat in plenty and be satisfied... (Joel 2:26).

Eat what? Have you ever wondered how Jesus could tell the disciples at the well in Samaria that He wasn't hungry because He had meat they knew nothing about? (See John 4:32.) Sometimes people are not hungry after preaching because they have eaten of the "meat" of the gospel. Or if they study the Word, all hunger has left because they have eaten of the "meat." It is a mystery that short circuits natural hunger. Jesus had meat to eat. His meat was to do the will of the Father, and He was satisfied. He didn't need common sustenance.

We have come into a season in the earth when tremendous disasters have been released, and there will be unprecedented lack in the world. But God has supernatural manna that will sustain His children. We are not going to lack in any area—physically, emotionally, spiritually, mentally, or financially.

The Lord asked me some time ago, "When are My people going to learn that finances are not an obstacle to accomplishing My will?" The Lord made the universe and all that it contains out of nothing, and we fret and worry about the "almighty" dollar. God will supernaturally invest in His work and in His people. He will make a way where the going looks absolutely impossible. But what is impossible with man, is possible with God. (Luke 18:27).

THE PLENTY OF GOD

You shall eat in plenty and be satisfied and praise the name of the Lord your God who has dealt wondrously with you. And My people shall never be put to shame. Then you shall know that I am in the midst of Israel (my people). *I am the Lord your God, and there is no other; My people shall never be put to shame* (Joel 2:26-27).

In a previous chapter, you read about Laban pursuing Jacob, and God warning Laban not to speak either good or bad. It was the Third Day. If we are purified, if we are holy, if we are without spot or wrinkle, if we are mature sons and daughters of God, the impure heart will not be able to speak against us. We are in that process, that place of change, so we will not be put to shame by our own foolishness. We will find that place of plenty in God where we will praise His name and declare His wondrous works!

After the outpouring of the former and latter rain together, on the first month, Joel declares the following: *"And it shall come to pass afterward that I will pour out My Spirit on all flesh. Your sons and daughters shall prophesy, your old men shall dream dreams and your young men will see visions. And also on My menservants and My maidservants, I will pour out My spirit in those days. And I will show wonders in the heavens and in the earth, blood and fire and pillars of smoke"* (Joel 2:28-30).

This passage contains revelation about the blood of Jesus, the purifying fire of God, and His magnificent glory. The earth is going to be filled with the knowledge of the glory of God. It will happen in supernatural ways spontaneously as the Lord sovereignly invades earth Himself as well as through His servants.

"The sun shall be turned to darkness..." declares Joel 2:31. We've always viewed that reference as the natural sunlight. But when the glory of God is so bright and shining on you that people need to wear sunglasses when close to you, the natural sun isn't that bright in comparison. Think big—God big. The glory of God is going to surpass and outshine the sun. That's the glory of God about to be released.

> *And it shall come to pass that whoever calls upon the name of the Lord shall be saved. For in Mount Zion and in Jerusalem there shall be deliverance...* (Joel 2:32).

Mount Zion and Jerusalem not only includes the Jewish people, but the Gentile believers as well. God's people, all of us, are included. There will be deliverance found in us for those who need help and cry out to God. That authority has been released. As we walk in the power of this Third Day revelation, demonized people will manifest around us even as we are walking down the street or in shopping malls. We will need to learn to hear from God before we react to what is happening around us. We will need to ask the Lord before we begin to deliver people. The timing of God is all-important in these matters. These types of situations will become more and more common until entire cities will be free of sickness, demons, immorality, and civil unrest. We will have cities of refuge where God, by His Spirit, will rule in totality and in reality.

Acts 3:19-21 says: *"Repent, therefore, and be converted, that your sins may be blotted out, so that times of refreshing may come from the presence of the Lord, and that He may send Jesus Christ, who has preached to you before, whom Heaven must receive until the times of restoration of all things, which God has spoken by the mouth of all of His holy prophets since the world began."*

Repent, be converted, have your sins blotted out so you can be refreshed. Believer and unbeliever have the same command. Restoration means "to bring back into existence or use, into the original condition." What's the original condition for man? Adam and Eve before the Fall. There will be no perfection here on this earth. But there will be maturity. Enoch walked with God. Enoch was a friend of God, and God took him. (Genesis 5:24). God is no respecter of persons. Remember Elijah was taken up as well. (2 Kings 2:11). These men had such passion for God that He brought them to Himself. Can we have that much passion? Yes!

To *restore* means, "to put back, to replace, to reinstate, to reinstall, to revive or recall to life, rebuild in a form of the original." The Lord will finish what He started. He has released to us in this hour gifts and a greater anointing to accomplish all that He desires. The fire of God is coming. Selfish ambition will be burned away. We will defer to one another, esteem one another, honor one another, and make room for one another. If you are not prepared for what He is about to release, you will miss out on one of the greatest expressions of the love of God you will ever know.

THE SHAKING

*On the next day, which followed the day of preparation, the chief priest and Pharisee gathered together to Pilate, saying, "Sir we remember while He was still alive how that deceiver said after three days I will rise. Therefore, command that the tomb be made secure until the **third day**. Lest the disciples come in the night and steal Him away and say to the people He has risen from the dead. So the last deception will be worst than the first." Pilate said to them "You have a guard, go your way, make it secure as you know how." So they went and made the tomb secure, sealing the stone and setting the guard. Now after the Sabbath, as the first day of the week began to dawn, Mary Magdalene and the other Mary came to see the tomb. And behold there was a great earthquake... (Matthew 27:62–28:2).*

Look at the portion that says, *"there was a great earthquake."* While I was resting at Ross Point in Idaho in December 2002, the Lord told me that there was going to be an earthquake, very shortly, of a magnitude seldom seen or recorded in modern times, and it was going to be a sign to us of greater birth pangs, to let us know that the end is very near. *A great earthquake.* On December 26, 2004, a magnitude 9.0 earthquake struck the 10/40 window in Southeast Asia. The devastation from that quake was beyond anything imaginable in modern times.

He also told me that there would be an assassination attempt on President George W. Bush that would be thwarted through intercession. In October 2004, numerous prayer networks from the Elijah List to numerous Capitol Hill and national prayer chains released an alert to pray for President Bush's safety against an assassination attempt. Any plan in that direction was thwarted by prayer.

> *A great earthquake…for an angel of the Lord descended from Heaven and came and rolled back the stone of the door and sat on it. His countenance was like lightening and his clothing as white as snow* (Matthew 28:1-3).

Many people in various meetings have witnessed flashes of light like lightening flashing across the room as the Lord confirms His Word. We cannot afford the luxury of rejecting these experiences just because they are outside the realm of our experience. We must, however, test every manifestation by the Word of God to be sure that we are not falling into error. But we cannot simply reject something because it has not been a part of our own limited experience in God. Most of the latter day workings of the Lord will be outside our realm of experience.

> *And the guards shook for fear of him and became like dead men. But the angel answered and said to the women "Do not be afraid, for I know that you seek Jesus who was crucified. He is not here for He has risen as He said. Come and see the place where He lay and go quickly and tell his disciples that He has risen from the dead and, indeed, He is going before you into Galilee. There you will see Him. Behold I have told you." So they went quickly from the tomb with fear and great joy and ran to bring his disciples the word* (Matthew 28:4-8).

Fear and great joy will be experienced by many in the church as the revelation of this resurrection power of Jesus is released throughout the earth. On the Third Day, resurrection life and power is being released. Jesus rose from the dead on the Third Day. He is a type and a forerunner of the Body. The resurrection life of God that is being released will transform the Church in such a way that the world will sit up and take note. The life of God is a life of health and vitality even in the midst of death and disease. The Church will experience what has for so long eluded them—divine health. There will not be found within the ranks of the army of God anyone who is feeble or sick.

Note that on the Third Day the seal was broken from off the stone and the stone was rolled away. This is significant and profound! The seal of end-time revelation and understanding has been broken. Jesus, the Word Himself, has come forth, and we are seeing a corresponding release of revelation, wisdom, and understanding not experienced before in the church. The Bible says that at the end of the age knowledge shall increase. For some reason we have always equated this to worldly knowledge, and that does have some truth in it. The greater weight of this Scriptural fulfillment, though, is in the fact that the knowledge of God is being released now as never before.

The Seals Opened

The Book of Daniel says it this way: "*Although I heard, I did not understand. Then I said, 'My Lord what shall be the end of these things?' And he said, 'Go your way, Daniel, for the words are closed up and sealed until the time of the end. Many shall be purified, made white and refined, without spot, without wrinkle. But the wicked shall do wickedly and none of the wicked shall understand but the wise will understand.'"* (Dan. 12:8-10).

Gross darkness shall cover the earth at the end of the age. Read Matthew 24:25. (Isaiah 60:2) There will be (is) wickedness, and mankind will be (is) involved in unspeakably vile things. But, those that are purified and made white and refined through the fire (see Lev. 7:17), are going to be partakers of and able to understand the revelation being released on this Third Day. We are a blessed and favored people just to be alive during this season of incredible fulfillment of the promises of God. We can choose to passionately pursue the Lord and fulfill our destiny or we can remain in the place of apathy and lethargy and miss the most incredible time in history. This is the time of destiny being released and you can participate in the greatest display of the Kingdom of Heaven ever released on earth. The choice is yours.

CHAPTER TWELVE

THE RELEASE

Resurrection Power and Life in a New Plan

Father, allow us to drink from the river of revelation and to receive insight regarding the hour in which we now live and the release of your Holy Spirit in our lives. I apply the blood of Jesus over the readers of this book, and I bind every hindering spirit that would try and cause confusion. We want to honor You in all we say and do, Father. We thank you in Jesus' name. Amen.

> *Now on the first day of the week, very early in the morning they and certain other women with them came to the tomb bringing the spices which they had prepared. But they found the stone rolled away from the tomb. Then they went in and did not find the body of the Lord Jesus. And it happened that they were greatly perplexed about that, and behold, two men stood by them in shining garments. Then, as they were afraid and bowed their faces to the earth, they said to them, "Why do you seek the living among the dead? He is not here but is risen! Remember how He spoke to you when He was still in Galilee saying: 'the Son of Man must be delivered into the hands of sinful men and be crucified and on the **third day** rise again.'" And they remembered*

His words. Then they returned from the tomb and told all these things to the eleven and to all the rest. It was Mary Magdalene, Joanna, Mary the mother of James, and the other women with them who told these things to the apostles. And their words seemed to them like idle tales and they did not believe them. But Peter arose and ran to the tomb; and stooping down, he saw the linen cloths lying by themselves; and he departed marveling to himself at what had happened (Luke 24:1-12).

AGAIN, EARLY IN THE MORNING ON THE THIRD DAY death was defeated. We have entered into a day/season of the release of resurrection life and power unlike any other time in history. The testimonies of multitudes being raised from the dead, many documented, some not, is awesome in scope. Why now? Why all of a sudden are we hearing about so many being raised from the dead in the last few years? It is the Third Day. The signs are all around us if we have eyes to see and ears to hear. *It is the Third Day!*

Correspondingly, there is also a release of incredible revelation as the "Word Himself" is coming forth out of the tomb of man's ignorance. Angelic visitation has increased on this Third Day, just as the prophetic picture depicts as we read of Mary and the other women having an angelic encounter at the garden tomb early in the morning on the Third Day. The prophetic promise for this hour is incredible!

THE PASSIONATE BELIEVER

Now behold two of them.... [Two who? Two disciples! Remember, two is the number of witness] *...were traveling that same day.* [They were on a journey. You and I are on a journey on this Third Day.] *They were traveling* *that same day to a village called Emmaus, which was about seven miles from Jerusalem. And they talked together of all these things which had happened* (Luke 24:13-14).

Emmaus means "to be hot from sunrise to sunset." There is a consistency of purpose and passion in relation to this verse that the Lord is calling us to on this Third Day. If we are to be partakers in the purposes of God in this hour we can no longer afford to vacillate between hot and cold, commitment and apathy, or truth and error. We must set our hearts to knowing Him and following Him, and we must forsake all worldly distractions that would hinder us from our pursuit of the destiny before us.

It is seven and a half miles between Emmaus and Jerusalem—seven is the number of completion, the finished product. And eight is the number of new beginnings. As a Church we are in the middle of a period of transition, moving from the second day paradigm and understanding of the Word of God into a new season. Few other Scriptures depict the transition in such a clear way as does this particular passage in Luke, which clearly indicates a season of change. It is the dawning of a new reformation that will see the culmination and fulfillment of the purposes of God for this earth and the coming of age of the church as a whole.

We cannot allow ourselves the luxury of falling back into the mundane and comfortable practices we've grown accustomed to in our Christian life. The tyranny of the familiar has always been the worst enemy of a fresh move of God and continues to be so. As the Word says in Hebrews 12:1, let us lay aside every weight, everything that would hinder us from embracing and walking in the fullness of the Spirit of God in the "now" of this season of incredible prophetic fulfillment.

So it was, while they conversed and reasoned, that Jesus Himself drew and went with them (Luke 24:15).

Why? The Word says in Matthew 18:20 where two or three are gathered together in His name, there He is in the midst. It could be rendered: where two or three of you are gathered in Christ-like *character*, there He is in the midst. Throughout the New Testament the word *name* means "character and authority"— in that order. If you are gathered together with Christ-like character, Christ-like authority will be imminent. It will be released.

But their eyes were restrained, so that they did not know Him (Luke 24:16).

There have been instances in each one of our lives when Jesus Himself was in our presence, but the circumstance or the grief or the doubt kept us from recognizing Him. Our eyes were not on the promise, but on the problem. This is an all too common malady within the Church. We must learn to keep our focus upon Jesus!

Take Peter for example. Peter challenged the Lord in Matthew 14:28 to command him to come to where the Lord was on the water. Peter was well on his way to where the Lord Jesus stood waiting for him when he began to notice the wind and the waves and the Scripture says he began to sink.

Peter's decline began the moment he took his eyes off of Jesus and put his eyes on the circumstance of the wind and the waves. Remember the boisterous windstorm that assailed Jesus and the disciples in Mark 4:35-41? When the disciples in their distress called upon Jesus, the Lord stood up and rebuked the wind and the waves, and there was a great calm.

This is a key to our overcoming in life: the authority of the Lord was demonstrated in the midst of dire need! We must learn to keep our eyes upon Jesus and understand that He is greater than any circumstance we might face.

> *And He said to them, "What kind of conversation is this that you had with one another as you walked and are sad?" Then one whose name was Cleopas answered and said to Him, "Are you the only stranger in Jerusalem and have you not known the things which happened there in these days?"* (Luke 24:17-18).

The name *Cleopas* is an interesting one. It means "called of God." Here is a picture of an individual, a believer, called of God, embarking on life's journey when Jesus shows up and is not recognized. Next, this follower of Jesus asks a question which on first glance appears to be utterly absurd, *"Are you the only stranger in Jerusalem and have you not known the things which happened there in these days?"*

Suffice it to say that Jesus was intimately acquainted with the events of the past few days. Rather, the questions reflect an attitude many Christians pose at one time or another during their walk; "Lord, are you a stranger to what I've been going through? Don't you know the things that have happened to me these past few days?"

> *And He said to them, "What things?" So they said to Him, "The things concerning Jesus of Nazareth, who was a Prophet mighty in deed and word before God and all the people, and how the chief priests and our rulers delivered Him to be condemned to death, and crucified Him. But we **were hoping** that it was He who was going to redeem*

Israel. Indeed, besides all this, today is **the third day** *since these things happened* (Luke 24:19-21).

The key to understanding why they did not recognize Jesus is in their comment "*...we were hoping...*" The disciples fell into the trap we all succumb to—they had a preconceived idea of how God was to accomplish His purposes on the earth. When Jesus didn't establish His Kingdom according to their understanding and reasoning, they lost sight of Him. It is our finite and misguided concept of an infinite God that causes us to measure Heaven and the God of Heaven by our earthly standards.

Rather than seek the Lord's wisdom and insight from a heavenly perspective, we try to bring Him down to our level of reason. The Third Day church must learn to rest in God and seek the heart of the Father and His strategies for the release of His Kingdom on this earth. We cannot afford the luxury of trying to cause the Lord to conform to *our* image any longer! We are to be conformed to *His* image and likeness! The Word is clear:

For as the heavens are higher than the earth, So are My ways higher than your ways, And My thoughts than your thoughts (Isaiah 55:9).

How then can we bridge the gap between where we are and where we are called to be? First Corinthians 2:16 says that we have the "*mind of Christ.*" We can learn to cultivate the unlimited wisdom of God by believing His Word and applying it to our lives.

New Sight in the Third Day

And certain women of our company who arrived at the tomb early astonished us. When they did not find his body, they came saying that they had also seen a vision of angels who said he was alive. Certain of those who were with us went to the tomb and found it just as the women had said. But him they did not see. Then he said to them "O foolish ones, slow of heart to believe in all that the prophets have spoken! Ought not the Christ to have suffered these things and to enter into his glory?" **And beginning with Moses and all the prophets, He expounded to them in all the Scriptures the things concerning himself** (Luke 24:22-27).

This prophetic picture is incredible! On this Third Day Jesus Himself will begin to open our understanding to receive revelation from His Word that will cause us to come to a place of intimacy and understanding of who He truly is, and it will also cause us to awaken to our destiny and the divine purpose of God for this generation. We must become lovers of the Word of God as well as lovers of the God of the Word! In so doing, we position ourselves for an incredible journey of discovery of the Lord Himself.

They drew near to the village where they were going and He indicated that He would have gone farther. But they constrained Him… (Luke 24:28-29).

This word *constrained* is a powerful word. It means "to force, compel, to have a burning fervency." It is a word that reflects passion! Only through a passionate desire and hunger for the Lord will we break the bonds of complacency and stagnation that have held us captive to a religious system devoid of life. Throughout the Bible we find that the Lord always responds to the passionate cry of a group or an individual—Moses, Abraham, Hagar, Jeremiah, Elijah, Peter, James, Mary (at the tomb) are only a few examples. Passion and fervency always gets the attention of and a response from Heaven, especially on this day when we are called to be "hot from sunrise to sunset."

> *But they constrained him saying "Abide with us for it is toward evening and the day is far spent." And He went in to stay with them. Now, it came to pass, as He sat at the table with them that He took bread, blessed and broke it and gave it to them…Then their eyes were opened and they knew Him. Then He vanished from their sight* (Luke 24:29-31).

Their eyes were opened and they were flooded with the intimacy they desired. Even though it was late evening, they ran all the way back to Jerusalem after the sun had set to tell the disciples that He is alive! It didn't matter how long it would take. It didn't matter the lateness of the hour. What mattered to them was telling the other disciples that Jesus was alive.

It doesn't matter the lateness of the hour when you receive a revelation of Jesus. Weariness will vanish, and a new zeal and passion will be birthed that will propel you toward your destiny. It says that these two disciples ran all the way back to tell the other disciples about their encounter with Jesus. I believe and pray that there will be a prophetic release right where you, the reader, are that will impregnate the atmosphere with the presence of the Lord and will release to you an encounter with His glorious presence. Just as Paul was three days without sight before Barnabas came and prayed for him, I also pray that on this Third Day your eyes will be opened to know Him!

> *And they* [disciples] *said to one another, "Did not our heart burn within us while He talked with us on the road and while He opened the Scriptures to us?" So they rose up*

that very hour, returned to Jerusalem and found the eleven and those who were with them gathered together saying, "The Lord has risen, indeed, and has appeared to Simon!" And they told about the things that had happened on the road and how He was known to them in the breaking of bread (Luke 24:32-35).

On this Third Day we have a prophetic promise: *our eyes will be opened, and we will know Him!* It is with a thankful heart and the breaking of bread that our revelation will come. As we worship the Lord and feed upon the living Word, we will come to know Him in ways we've never dared dream. This release of revelation is spoken of in Scripture:

But you, Daniel, shut up the words, and seal the book until the time of the end; many shall run to and fro, and knowledge shall increase (Daniel 12:4).

This is the end of the age, and knowledge is increasing. This increase is not going to be only in the areas of science and technology, but the knowledge of God—the God kind of knowledge will increase!

THE RELEASE OF THE NEW WINE

*Now, on the **third day** there was a wedding in Cana of Galilee and the mother of Jesus was there. Now both Jesus and His disciples were invited to the wedding and when they ran out of wine the mother of Jesus said to Him, "They have no wine." Jesus said to her, "Woman, what does your concern have to do with Me? My hour has not yet come." His mother said to the servants, "Whatever He says to you, do it." Now there were set there six waterpots of stone,*

*according to the manner of purification of the Jews, con-
taining twenty or thirty gallons apiece.* (John 2:1-6).

(We know that *six* is the number of man. The waterpots
made of stone speak of the dust of the earth—flesh. There are six
waterpots sitting there empty. They can each hold 20 to 30 gallons apiece. *Twenty* is the number of divine order. It means to
divide, to judge and it speaks of holiness. Thirty speaks of maturity and sonship. The waterpots are empty—that's us.)

*Jesus said to them, "Fill the waterpots with water," and
they filled them up to the brim. And He said to them,
"Draw some out now, and take it to the master of the feast."
And they took it. When the master of the feast had tasted
the water that was made wine, and did not know where it
came from, (but the servants who had drawn the water
knew), the master of the feast called the bridegroom. And
he said unto him, "Every man at the beginning sets out the
good wine and when the guests are well drunk, then the
inferior. You have kept the good wine until now!"* (John
2:7-10).

THE BEST WINE RESERVED UNTIL THE THIRD DAY

Here is the Kingdom principle of producing new wine.
Continually fill yourself with the water of the Word of God.
When you are full, in faith you begin to pour forth that which
you have received. As you actively release your faith, the best wine
comes forth. These stone pots were created to carry water. We
who are called to be vessels of God were created to carry the water
of His Word. Notice Jesus didn't say to pick out the vessels that
have been to the best schools or only those who are in ministry.

Again, six is the number representing all people in Scripture, therefore we all qualify! These were common, ordinary stone waterpots. The principle is clear; we must fill ourselves with the Word of God, and we are then prepared to be poured forth as Jesus directs. When we are obedient, the best wine will come forth.

This beginning of signs Jesus did in Cana and Galilee and manifested His glory and His disciples believed in Him (John 2:11).

Or do you not know that your body is the temple of the Holy Spirit, who is in you, whom you have from God? You are not your own? For you were bought at a price; therefore, glorify God in your body and in your spirit which are God's (1 Corinthians 6:19-20).

Who do you belong to? God! Glorify God in your body and in your spirit. We glorify God by recognizing His Lordship or His authority in our life by doing what He says. Do you know it is worship when you turn to God and say, "God, I don't know what to do"? The most effective way for a believer to worship and glorify God in our bodies is to allow Him through our weakness to become strong. Obedience to the mandate of Heaven—the voice of God—is an act of worship that says, "I love you Lord." There is a divine exchange that takes place that is a mystery to every Christian—the love of the Father that grants us grace to accomplish His will with His wisdom and His strength in the midst of our weakness.

We can be filled with the water of His Word. We can allow the Lord to direct us and to pour forth that which He has labored to impart to us. In so doing we will see the results of obedience—the best wine at last. Let's return to John 2:13:

> *Now the Passover of the Jews was at hand, and Jesus went up to Jerusalem. And He found in the temple those who sold oxen and sheep and doves, and the money changers doing business. When He had made a whip of cords, He drove them all out of the temple, with the sheep and the oxen, and poured out the changers' money and overturned the tables. And He said to those who sold doves, "Take these things away! Do not make My Father's house a house of merchandise!" Then His disciples remembered that it was written, "Zeal for Your house has eaten Me up." So the Jews answered and said to Him, "What sign do You show to us, since You do these things?" Jesus answered and said to them, "Destroy this temple, and in three days I will raise it up." Then the Jews said, "It has taken forty-six years to build this temple, and will You raise it up in three days?"*

Jesus was speaking of the temple of His Body. We are that temple! On the Third Day, He will raise us up with Him. However there is a work of cleansing that will take place at the same time. The Lord will drive the "money changers" out of His temple, and we will become once again a people of prayer. The idols that we have erected in our hearts before the Lord will be dealt with in a manner that is both effective and final. We can be encouraged that in this hour Jesus Himself will be working in us both to do His will and to do of His good pleasure.

First Corinthians 12:13 says: "*For by one Spirit we are all baptized into one body—whether Jews or Greeks, whether slave or free—and have all been made to drink into one Spirit.*"

I am Canadian, American, Chinese, Fijian, Indian, Jewish, Arab, etc. I am a member in particular of one body—the Body of Christ! It does not matter the label you put on me; Methodist, Pentecostal, Baptist, Presbyterian, Catholic, Lutheran, etc. If we have confessed Jesus as our Lord and Savior we are one. On this Third Day the "unity of the faith" is going to become a major sign to the rest of the world that the Lord is at work within His Body. We will become one Body—in focus, in passion, and in character! Our focus will be the great harvest; our passion will be to become more like Jesus, and our character will be conformed to Christ-like character.

> *But know, indeed, there are many members, yet one body. ...Now you are the body of Christ, and members individually* (1 Corinthians 12:20,27).

We've been too individual. We've kept our individuality and exalted it to the extent that we will not allow ourselves to be one. We can keep our personality, but we need to lose the "me first," selfish, self-centered place. It's not all about me. *There's only one individual in the Kingdom—Jesus!*

In Acts 10:40-41 it says: "*Him God raised up on the **third day** and showed Him openly, **not to all the people**, but to witnesses chosen before by God; even to us who ate and drank with Him after He arose from the dead.*"

We will be witnesses of the resurrected Jesus. Many people are experiencing visitations from the Lord Jesus Himself in this day. The Bible says *not to all the people.* Here is the key: the witnesses were chosen before by God, and they were those who ate and drank with Him after He arose from the dead. As believers we recognize it is the death, burial, and resurrection of the Lord Jesus that allows us access to the Father—we are born again. We have the privilege to eat His flesh (the Word of God) and to drink His blood, (our covenant promises in the Word), and by so doing we are positioned by this relationship to become eyewitnesses of Jesus Himself.

Jesus is no respecter of persons. Is the desire of your heart to see Him? On the Third Day, many of you will. You have the same access to the Holy of Holies as every believer in the past and present. You can and will experience visions and revelations of the Lord on this day. You will increase and grow in the revelation and understanding of Jesus on this day. You can participate in the greatest move of God the world has ever witnessed on this day. All of these Third Day promises are yours if you will receive the revelation of what the Lord desires to impart to His Body in this hour! This is the hour of your destiny being fulfilled!

A New Structure on the Third Day

In Acts 27, we read the story of Paul's journey to Rome. Paul had been compelled by reason of persecution from his own people to appeal to Caesar in Rome. It becomes evident during Paul's journey that the Lord's plans are not man's plans. God had a different route to Rome for Paul because there was a need for the gospel to be preached on a remote island called Malta.

> *When much time had been spent and sailing was now dangerous because the Fast was already over, Paul advised them saying, "Men, I perceive that this voyage will end with disaster and much loss not only of the cargo and ship but also our lives." Nevertheless, the centurion was more persuaded by the helmsman and the owner of the ship than by the things spoken by Paul. And because the harbor was not*

suitable to winter in, the majority advised to set sail from there also, if by any means they could reach Phoenix, a harbor of Crete opening to the southwest and northwest and winter there (Acts 27:9-12).

Paul had been praying and fasting when the Lord visited Him and warned him of imminent disaster if they proceeded on the course they had set. The centurion chose to listen to the helmsman (the ship's captain) and the owner of the ship rather than the prophet of God. From a logical standpoint (man's logic), it was the right decision to make. The circumstances indicated that change was necessary—the harbor was not suitable to winter in—and the experts agreed that it would be wiser to sail farther. The board (the majority) made a recommendation that the ship should set sail for a better harbor.

When the south wind blew softly supposing that they had obtained their desire, putting out to sea, they sailed close by Crete. But not long after a tempestuous head wind arose called Euroclydon, [which means a northeaster]. So when the ship was caught and could not head into the wind, we let her drive. And running into the shelter of an island called Clauda, we secured the skiff with difficulty. When they had taken it on board they used cables to undergird the ship and fearing lest they should run aground on the Syrtis Sands, they struck sail and so were driven (Acts 27:13-17).

Let's examine this Scripture in light of the Third Day. The vessel Paul was on is a type of the second day church model with all of its familiar attributes: the same programs, traditions, doctrines, and order of worship we've always known. Everything is status quo when the Word of the Lord is declared through His servant that He has a new and different strategy.

It is unfortunate that the Church as a whole has become so enmeshed in the tyranny of the familiar that change is an abhorrent concept. Too often we hold meetings and take votes as to what we should do in any given situation rather than seek God for His vision and strategy for us. The soft south wind that blew around Paul's ship is a picture of the love of the Father as He releases His Holy Spirit to lead and guide us into our destiny. Even though those onboard the ship "Second Day Model" had a course set, God in His wisdom had a course change for them, and He wasn't going to allow them to stay in that place of "Church as Usual" (sailing as we've always done). As we transition from what we have known as "church" to a new Third Day model we can no longer hold to our familiar Madison Avenue Marketing Techniques and Church Growth Strategies. We must allow God to direct our steps and set our course.

And because we were exceedingly tempest tossed, the next day they lightened the ship (Acts 27:18).

The Most High will have His way in this day. You'll notice, slowly, church leaders are beginning to throw out the programs, the things that aren't working anymore. Pastors and leaders who have tried to pattern themselves after man and what God has done in other sectors of Christianity will not make any headway in this move of God as the Wind of the Spirit is released in the Church.

We must all do as Paul did; fast and pray for direction. Our destinies, while focused on building His Kingdom, are also unique, and we need a fresh strategy from Heaven to accomplish all that He is calling us to. We cannot afford the luxury of our modern day spiritual idolatry by continually trying to emulate another's successful church program. In doing so, we make ourselves in the image of a man and not The Man—Jesus. The Lord is challenging us with a fresh new wind of His Spirit—a new release from Heaven—that will propel us toward our destiny if we will trust Him.

PIONEERS IN GOD

*On the **third day**, we threw the ship's tackle overboard with our own hands* (Acts 27:19).

It is time to lighten the load. It is time to take all of our preconceived ideas and strategies of man and throw them overboard. It is time to rely totally upon the wind of the Spirit of God to blow, to carry us wherever He wants us to go. If we continue to try to hold onto the second day paradigm, the second day wine skin, or the second day strategy, we're going to end up shipwrecked...and some of us will die.

Those who received strategies from God in the past and built the ministries we recognize today are not part of that warning. There are some tremendous things that God established and laid as a foundation for us to build upon in this hour. They are foundations for us, but the plan for us is different in this day. We have been created for change. The only thing in the universe that doesn't change is God. We must trust the Lord and learn to abandon ourselves to the Holy Spirit in this hour. He will lead us and guide us to that place the Lord desires for us to be. He has called us to be pioneers, not settlers.

A pioneer is one who is on a journey of discovery. Each day is a new challenge with new strategies and greater insight into the will of the Father. What would church be like if each week we chose to lay aside our routine programs and allow the Lord to move in anyway He desires? What if our only program was to come and sit at His feet and wait upon Him to move upon us as we worship Him? What would church be like if the only predisposition we had was a heart of expectancy and anticipation? What could the Lord do in an atmosphere of total dependence upon Him rather than our feeble structures and traditions? This is not to say that all such structures and traditions are wrong. Some of them are even ordered by God. Most of them, however, are ordered despite God.

> *Now when neither sun nor stars appeared for many days and no small tempest beat upon us, all hope that we would be saved was finally given up. But after a long abstinence from food, then Paul stood in the midst of them and said, "Men, you should have listened to me and not have sailed from Crete and incurred this disaster and loss. And now I urge you to take heart, for there will be no loss of life among you, but only of the ship. For there stood by me this night an angel of the God to whom I belong and whom I serve saying, 'Do not be afraid, Paul; you must be brought before Caesar; and indeed God has granted you and all who sail with you.' Therefore take heart, men, for I believe God that it will be just as it was told me"* (Acts 27:20-25).

We would do well to memorize Acts 27:25. *"Therefore take heart, men, for I believe God that it will be just as it was told me."* Paul, who received the initial warning and perceived that there was disaster in the making, fasted and prayed on behalf of those who took him right into the jaws of death. He didn't accuse them. He didn't rail against them. He interceded! He interceded on their behalf, and the Lord came and promised him that all would live with only the loss of the ship.

They still would have done it their own way, except the Centurion recognized that Paul was right. Some of them tried to take the life boat, throw it in the water and escape. But Paul declared that if they tried to use it, all would die. So the Centurion cut off the lifeboat and commanded them to stay with the ship as it broke apart. The ship ran aground on the island of Malta. Every life was spared. The wind of God took them to that island by His divine strategy and direction...and Malta had a revival.

What if we just throw out our programs and allow God to do whatever He wants to do every time we get together? What if we see revival break out everywhere we go, just because we trust God? On the Third Day, this command is clear—trust God! Let's throw ourselves upon His mercy. Let's willingly allow the Spirit of God to take us wherever He wants. Let's abandon ourselves to God in this hour and see the amazing things He will do!

So let's review the promises of the Third Day:

There is a separation taking place, and it is by the Hand of God—that which is flesh and that which is spirit.

Watch what you say, because there will be a *quick harvest of what we release.*

We must learn to *love the God of the promise* more than the promise of God.

We must allow the purification of our lives so that *all flesh is burned away.*

Those of *an impure heart will no longer be able to speak either good or evil into our lives.*

The outpouring of the *former and latter rains will come together* on the Third Day, releasing visitation, power, and many supernatural manifestations.

We will *retrieve all that has been stolen from us, plus the spoils.*

Like Esther, *we will be raised up to stand in the gap for the nation, to see a nation saved. It is our purpose* to be a part of the final harvest.

The temple will be completed on the Third Day.

Resurrection life is released to raise this Body up! That's us! Jesus will be found in the temple, and *we will have an encounter with the Living God that will radically transform our lives.*

God has bestowed upon us, this generation, the greatest of all honors: to see Him bring to a conclusion everything He began from Adam until now. He has chosen us to be partakers of the final victory, the overcoming power of Almighty God, the release of His glory on the earth. *On the Third Day His glory will come down and be seen upon His people.* If you are willing, just say yes to Him and it is accomplished. If you say, "Yes," He says "Amen."

He is waiting for us right now to cry out to Him and say, "Yes, Lord!" to the promise of the Third Day. This is your destiny; whether you are 10 or 100, educated or uneducated, short, tall, skinny—it doesn't matter. If you are willing and obedient, the promises of the Third Day belongs to you!

Father, You have laid an incredible journey before us. Your Word has taken us through the destiny that you have for Your people—we can't fully comprehend this destiny Father, because we have nothing with which to compare it. Father, we know that these few Scriptures are only a tiny tip of Your iceberg, and that this revelation continually unfolds before us. Father, I'm asking for a special impartation into the people who read this book—graft this Word into their spirits.

Jesus, you said on the Third Day you appeared to certain ones. Grant that these would be the certain ones, Lord, that You would visit Your people face to face that they might know You as they've never known You before. Let them be transformed—make it obvious that though we are an unlearned and ignorant people, we have been with You.

Lord, I thank you for visitation, impartation, and activation. But mostly, Father, I thank You for Your heart toward the readers. We love you, Lord, and you are worthy of all honor and all glory.

Pray this with me: Father help me by an act of my will, to throw out my ship's tackle. Every preconceived idea or notion, every program, I release and ask for Your agenda, your plan. Father, I throw them out and abandon my soul to Your Spirit, in Jesus' name.

Thank you, Father.

Amen!

ABOUT THE AUTHOR

THROUGHOUT THE YEARS, many churches, cities, and nations have been touched and inspired by the life-changing power of God flowing through Bruce Allen.

Gifted in the prophetic and teaching ministry, the Lord uses Bruce to impart, activate, and release individuals and churches into deeper realms of the Spirit. A compelling presence of the Holy Spirit permeates the atmosphere, and it is not unusual for unique signs, wonders, and miracles to flow freely in each meeting.

The Father Heart of God is evidenced in Bruce's ministry as the presence and glory of the Lord is released drawing many back to the Father and causing many to draw deeply from the well of His presence.

The mandate of *Still Waters International* is to "Prepare the way of the Lord and make straight paths for His feet." This mandate focuses not only on the soon return of the Lord, but also for those who have been hungering for the presence of God in a deeper way in their life.

Still Waters International
PO Box 1001 Chewelah, WA 99109
Phone 509-340-1369
E-mail abidesinrest@msn.com
Website www.stillwatersinternational.org

Additional copies of this book and other
book titles from DESTINY IMAGE are
available at your local bookstore.

Call toll-free: 1-800-722-6774.

Send a request for a catalog to:

Destiny Image® **Publishers, Inc.**
P.O. Box 310
Shippensburg, PA 17257-0310

"Speaking to the Purposes of God for This
Generation and for the Generations to Come"

For a complete list of our titles,
visit us at www.destinyimage.com